# 荒原·情歌
The Waste Land/The Love Song of J. Alfred Prufrock

中英对照 世纪译本

# 荒原·情歌

*The Waste Land*
*The Love Song of J. Alfred Prufrock*

【英】T.S.艾略特 著

陶志健 译

Acer Books

荒原·情歌（中英对照）（红枫丛书之一）
作者：T.S.艾略特
汉译：陶志健
摄影：陶志健
出版：Acer Books

书号：978-1-7381938-1-3


红枫丛书
策划：黎杨
设计：陶志健


The Waste Land/The Love Song of J. Alfred Prufrock
Author: T.S. Eliot
Chinese Translator: Tao, Zhijian
Cover Photo: Zijian
Publisher: Acer Books

ISBN: 978-1-7381938-1-3


Copyright © 2024 Tao Zhijian.

All rights reserved. No part of this book, except contents in the public domain, may be reproduced or used in any manner without the prior written permission of the copyright owner, except for the use of brief quotations in critical articles and book reviews.

E-mail: acerbookscanada@gmail.com

# 目 录

目 录 ................................................................. i
前 言 ................................................................ iii
荒 原 ................................................................. 1
 一、葬亡 ......................................................... 1
 二、棋局 ......................................................... 7
 三、火诫 ........................................................ 12
 四、溺亡 ........................................................ 19
 五、雷之语 ...................................................... 20
 作者原注 ........................................................ 27
The Waste Land ..................................................... 41
 I. The Burial of the Dead ..................................... 41
 II. A Game of Chess ........................................... 44
 III. The Fire Sermon .......................................... 48
 IV. Death by Water ............................................ 54
 V. What the Thunder Said ...................................... 54
 NOTES ......................................................... 59
《荒原》翻译要点 ..................................................... 67
J.阿尔弗雷德·普鲁弗洛克的情歌 ........................................ 84
The Love Song of J. Alfred Prufrock ................................ 93
《情歌》好唱口难开 .................................................. 100

i

## 目录

附录 .................................................................. 106
   当可爱的女人失足犯傻 ............................. 106
   When Lovely Woman Stoops to Folly ................. 107
   致他的忸怩女友 ......................................... 108
   To His Coy Mistress ....................................... 110
译后记 ................................................................ 115

# 前　言

　　书房的窗外，雪花飞扬，一片寂静，一片茫茫。这是 2022 年元月 2 日，昨晚刚改毕《荒原》译本第三稿。打算放一放，再进一步搜寻参考资料，进一步深入，进一步细化。从动笔到现在，两个月过去了。站在窗前，看着雪飘，我在自问：我是怎么搞到要翻译这首以晦涩著称的英美现代诗歌里程碑的？这本是想都不敢想的事啊！

　　好像还是要从读诗开始。这大疫流行之冬，大雪覆盖之下，除了含饴弄孙，还有很多时间可以读一点什么——哦，好像也可以借着雪盖"浑然忘世"（《荒原》）。读着，就唤醒了大概是做翻译做出的毛病：每读原著，都情不自禁地要对照一下译作，一是为吃透原作而参考，二是看人家如何信达。反过来也一样，读译著时常想回头对照原文。得益之余，也每每见到令人疑惑与不尽如人意之处，或时而如我所料，见到译者陷入英文的坑中。译得好的，心中佩服，就过去了；译得不如意的，总觉不适，想一改为快。一边读着，一边就将所读版本中有疑问、不如意之处重新试译；不知不觉，就扩大了搜寻研究资料的范围，也就扩大了翻译的篇幅。一来二去，索性走上了全文翻译的不归之路——似乎有些不知深浅了。

## 前言

《荒原》原作发表已经整整一个世纪了，也已出现前人多个中文译本。前人是高山，如第一个翻译这首诗的赵萝蕤先生，可谓巨人。想到她当年一个二十多岁的在校生，竟能作出如此雄文，真不是浪得虚名；读到的还有查良铮（诗人穆旦）和汤永宽两个译本，都是力作，令人钦佩。其他译本，限于中文资料的一时匮乏，未能有幸一一拜读（四月回国隔离期间又购得赵毅衡和裘小龙两个译本的电子版，得以匆匆览读）。

敬仰之余，也发现许多问题，或者说令人疑惑之处，反映了这首诗给翻译造成的困难之大。一部作品无非是内容和形式两个方面，二者水乳交融，互为依存。而翻译首先是对此二者的深刻理解和充分体察，进而才有可能尽好地再现原作。前者的难点涉及语言、文化、背景、语境、意境等。而上述令人疑惑之处，有个别属于低级错误，有些则实为硬译，还有些浮于字面而失却了原诗的丰厚内涵和内在逻辑，究其原因，都可以从理解体验方面探寻。例如全诗第一段中时态的变化及其时序的内涵，未见有任何译本能够明察并再现，因而读起来就缺乏了事态的层次感和通透感。另如，诗中"wisest woman"的"wise"一词旧有"通巫术、通神、有魔力"之义，妙用文中，富含深意，简单译作"智慧"则失之浅缺，且有违语境。

再者，既然是诗，就有诗的味道，无论是古典的，还是现代的。那么译诗也应该尽力再现其诗的味道。具体到《荒原》，诗中的修辞手法和表现手段众多，仅从韵律上看，尽管不是全文齐整，也广泛使用了包括各种节奏和韵律的多种手法。这些"诗素"及其所达成的"诗意"不仅在阅读时值得关注和欣赏，在译文中也值得尽量转达。比如作品中嵌入的几首变体十四行诗（sonnet），也未见得到任何译本的体察和关注。由于这种外在形式从未得到认识和再现，其所含的内在意味也因此未能得到充分挖掘和转达，"信"和"达"在这两个层面上便都暴露出余地。"雅"则另当别论。

如上所举的例子，原作中还有很多，其深厚的蕴涵值得我们仔细探究。这本册子后面附有另文《〈荒原〉翻译要点》，对翻译中所碰到的各类问题详加讨论。

本册还包含了艾略特的另一首诗，即他第一首正式发表的《J. 阿尔弗雷德·普鲁弗洛克的情歌》。这首诗的翻译，也是基于同样的考量，并采用了同样的标准。后面也附有翻译手记加以讨论。

如今我们站在巨人肩上，得益良多；同时今天我们有着非常方便的研究和资料搜寻条件，身居英语国家尤其如此；我们有理由有责任能看得更远些，体味更深些，转达更多些原作的深义和诗意，才不辜负巨人的肩，也不辜负时代所赐。译者为此做了大量的探索和斟酌，辛苦而快乐。至于眼前这个译本在何等程度上做出了新的贡献，还有待专家学者以及广大读者评鉴。

毕竟原作鸿篇巨帙，笔力雄厚，诗风浩荡，自如地驰骋于欧洲文学名篇之林，以笔者之才疏学浅，尽管发现了前人译本中颇多可商榷之处，并做了诸多努力加以改进，竭力传达原诗韵味，然而翻译过程也深感力有不逮，译本中难免仍有各种瑕疵，还要恳请各位读者方家不吝指正，以使经典名著的中译本不断完善。

在此，我要感谢前文提到的各位翻译家，是他们的

## 前言

辛勤劳作和所贡献的译本为我的译本提供了雄厚的参照。他们都是我尊敬的间接师长。翻译过程中，涉及《奥义书》的内容，曾向中国社科院亚太研究院研究员刘建老师请益，得到悉心指导，同时也在译文文字方面征得宝贵意见；去年（2022年）5月受邀在山西大学外语学院讲座谈《荒原》翻译，与老师同学们的讨论也使我受到启发；另，承蒙加拿大《华侨新报》黎杨主编推荐拙译《荒原》在所编周报连载刊登；我谨在此一并表达由衷的谢意。

翻译家柳鸣九认为，经典作品应该允许重译，而且必须重译；一部世界经典名著在某个国家在某个民族中出现一个理解得最准确、最透彻，再现得最神形相似、最流畅、最文采飞扬的译本，正是一代一代学人，一个一个研究者，一个一个译者逐渐积累、逐渐加工、逐渐精雕细刻而成的。如果能够跻身他们之中，为这样一个译本汇入点滴，将是我的荣幸。

2022年元月——2023年9月，蒙特利尔

# 荒　原[1]

"因我曾亲眼看见库迈的西比拉吊在一只罐子里，当孩子们问她'西比拉，你想要咋样？'她回答，'我想死。'"[a]

献给埃兹拉·庞德
艺高一筹[b]

## 一、葬亡

四月之月最是残酷，把
丁香在那死地上滋育，把

---

[a] 原文为拉丁文夹希腊文，出自一世纪小说家盖厄斯·佩特罗尼乌斯·阿尔比特作品《萨蒂里孔》中的人物 Encolpius 之口："NAM sibyllam quidem Cuimis ego ipse oculis meis vidi in ampulla pendere, et cum illi pueri dicerent: Σιβνλλατιθελειζ; repondebat illa: αποθαν ειν θελω."西比拉即女先知，而库迈的西比拉是希腊神话中最有名的女先知。她得到阿波罗的恩赐，可享如一抔土中的颗粒数那样的长寿，却未能得到青春，故于老朽之年渴求死亡。

　　另，英文原诗中出现的外文，无论在原文中是否以斜体出现，译本都用楷体表示；所有脚注均为译者所加，以字母标注；诗人原作尾注在译文中仍作尾注，增加数字标注，必要处在原注后附译者按，提供详情或解释。

[b] 原文为意大利文："il miglior fabbro"（引自但丁《神曲·炼狱篇》第26首）。

记忆和欲望搅作一团,把

麻木的根用春雨拨弄。

5 冬天保了我们温暖,把

大地盖上忘世的雪,把

一丝生机用枯茎喂养。ᵃ

夏天给了我们一惊,掠过施塔恩贝格湖

携雨而至;我们在柱廊里稍候,

10 接着在阳光下,走进王宫花园,ᵇ

喝着咖啡,聊了一个小时。

我可不是俄罗斯人,我来自立陶宛,正宗日耳曼人ᶜ

我们小时候,在大公家小住,ᵈ

就是表兄家,他带我去滑雪橇,

---

ᵃ 参见詹姆士·汤姆森(James Thomson)《致死亡诸女神》(*To Our Ladies of Death*)中的诗句:"母亲养育了我们幼小的生命,使我们能以死反哺于她。"("Our Mother feedeth thus our little life/That we in turn may feed her with our death.")

ᵇ 施塔恩贝格湖:慕尼黑南面一片湖,巴伐利亚国王同性恋者路德维希二世的尸体于湖中找到;王宫花园:慕尼黑城内一座公园。

ᶜ 原文为德文:"Bin gar keine Russin, stamm' aus Litauen, echt deutsch",在原诗中没有用斜体。其中"Russin"是阴性,表明叙述者是女性,人物原型当是玛丽·路易斯·拉里施伯爵夫人,即第15行中的"玛丽",艾略特称曾与她会面。这一段的情节与拉里施伯爵夫人的回忆录《我的过去》(*My Past*)中的叙述相吻合。

ᵈ 大公:可能指奥匈帝国皇储鲁道夫,因婚姻不幸,精神崩溃,与情妇一同自杀身亡;或指皇储弗朗茨·斐迪南大公,在萨拉热窝被塞尔维亚王国民族主义者普林西普刺杀身亡,成为第一次世界大战的导火线。

15 我很害怕。他说,玛丽,
玛丽,手抓牢啊。我们便一冲而下。
在大山里,真是自由自在。
我读书读个大半夜,冬天就去南方。

是什么根紧抓这烂石堆,什么枝[a]
20 从这烂石堆中长出来?人子啊,[2]
你说不出,猜不到,因为你所见只是
一堆破碎景象,那里烈日暴晒,
死树不给遮庇,蟋蟀不给宽慰,[3]
干石头不发出一丝水声。只是
25 这红色岩石之下才有庇荫,[b]
(来吧,钻进这红岩下的庇荫),
我要给你看一样东西,既不像
早晨在身后随你迈步的影子,
也不像傍晚升起迎你的影子;
30 我要给你看一抔尘土中的恐惧。[c]

　　清风习习地吹呀

---

[a] 参阅《圣经·旧约·约伯记》第 8 章第 17 节:"他的根盘绕石堆,钻入石缝。"
[b] 参阅《圣经·旧约·以赛亚书》第 32 章:"必有一人像避风所,和避暴雨的隐密处,像干旱之地的溪水,又像疲乏之地的大盘石的阴影。"
[c] 一抔尘土:参见题词的脚注;另一说认为"一抔尘土"来自约翰·邓恩的《祈祷集》(*Devotions*);第三种解释认为与英国国教葬亡祭词"尘归尘,土归土"相关。

 荒原

吹到我家乡
我那爱尔兰姑娘呀
你流连在何方？4

35　"一年前你第一次送我风信子；
　　"他们都叫我风信子姑娘。"a
　　——可我们很晚从风信子园回来时，
　　你两臂满抱，湿着头发，我却说不
　　出话，眼睛也看不见，我既不
40　活又不死，什么也不知道，
　　凝望着光亮的深处，一片寂静。b
　　荒凉空寂是那大海。5


　　梭梭垂斯夫人，那有名的慧眼，c
　　患了重感冒，尽管如此

---

a 风信子姑娘：希腊神话中阿波罗爱上斯巴达王的儿子海厄森斯（Hyacinth）却不幸导致他死亡，后以"风信子"纪念他，故传统上风信子代表美男子。这几行有两层含义：1.荒原之中，纯爱已死；2.影射男女不辨和变态性爱（这些在当时是不"正确"的）的无力无能。

b 从38行到41行的各个词句或情景皆出自但丁《神曲》《地狱篇》和《天堂篇》两篇的尾章，暗喻现代荒原中爱情的瘫痪及其被救赎的可能性。另，评者论"光亮的深处（heart of light）"或与约瑟夫·康拉德的 heart of darkness 有深层联系。

c 梭梭垂斯：由赫胥黎（Aldous Huxley）小说《铭黄》（*Crome Yellow*）中女巫师 Sesostris 的名字衍生而来。书中斯科根先生（Scogan）冒名 Sesostris 扮作吉普赛女巫师，在集市上算命。普遍认为其原型是哲学家伯特兰·罗素。赫胥黎与罗素多有交集，前者把他对后者的印象注入人物斯科根加以讽刺。

45　仍被认作欧洲最通神的女人，
　　手握一副诡妙的纸牌。这张，她说，[6]
　　是你的牌，淹死的腓尼基水手，[a]
　　（那些明珠原是他的眼睛。瞧啊！）[b]
　　这张是贝拉东纳，岩间女士，[c]
50　那位随情就景的女士。
　　这张是持三根权杖者，这张是转轮，[d]
　　这张是独眼商人，而这张牌[e]
　　空白一张，是他背在背上
　　不让我看的。我找不到
55　那张倒悬者。当心溺亡水中。[f]

---

[a] 参见第四部分"溺亡"中的弗莱巴，联系下文"当心溺亡水中"。

[b] 见莎士比亚《暴风雨》第一幕第二场中爱丽儿唱的丧歌（朱生豪译）："五浔的水深处躺着你的父亲，他的骨骼已化成珊瑚；他眼睛是耀眼的明珠；他消失的全身没有一处不曾受到海水神奇的变幻，化成瑰宝，富丽而珍怪。"

[c] "贝拉东纳（Belladonna）"一词源于意大利语 bella donna，意为"漂亮女人"，是一种植物（颠茄），可制眼用化妆品，也是毒药，其中"donna"含圣母之意；"岩间女士（the Lady of the Rocks）"暗指达芬奇作品《岩间圣母》（Virgin of the Rocks）和《蒙娜丽莎》（Mona Lisa）；在下一行又转成"那位随情就景的女士"，综合起来，应该代表了诗中各种情景下的女性人物。参见原注第218行。

[d] "持三根权杖者"：见原注第46行；转轮：即命运转轮。

[e] 独眼商人：即第三节"火诫"里贩卖葡萄干的尤金尼德斯先生。"独眼"是卡上的形象，暗示无良、罪恶或海盗。

[f] "倒悬者"与"雷之语"中"罩着头的人"相通。他象征丰产之神的自我牺牲，以便在重生之日为大地带来丰产。因为他"罩着头"，所以梭梭垂斯夫人看不到他。

我看到成群的人，围成圈子走动。
谢谢。你若见到亲爱的艾奎通太太[a]
请告诉她我亲自带着星象图：
这年头是要格外谨慎的呀。

60  诡异的城啊，[7]
在冬日拂晓的褐色雾中，
一群人流过伦敦桥，那么多人，
没想到死神竟报废了那么多人。[8]
叹息，短促的叹息，偶而嘘出，[9]
65  每个人的眼睛都锁定在脚前。
流上街坡又流下威廉王大街，
流到圣玛丽·伍尔诺斯教堂[b]
敲响九点钟最后沉死的一响。[10]
我看到一个熟人，喊住了他："斯特森！[c]
70  你，在迈利和我在一个舰队的！[d]

---

[a] 艾奎通太太：一说诗人用艾奎通代表他所讨厌的妻子薇薇恩。传闻罗素与薇薇恩有染，此处暗讽二人。参阅第43行脚注。

[b] 圣玛丽·伍尔诺斯教堂位于"伦敦城"（即伦敦金融区），被"报废了"的现代人群按时按点"流"入该区上班。

[c] "斯特森（Stetson）"：其来源有几说：或艾略特银行同事的名字，或艾略特的朋友埃兹拉·庞德（常戴斯特森帽），或伦敦一家帽商的字号，因很多人戴这家商铺的帽子，因而泛指任何人。

[d] 迈利：西西里一海港。公元前260年，罗马在迈利附近赢得对迦太基的重要海战。能遇见千年以前死亡战友的场所暗

去年你栽在花园里的尸体，a
开始发芽了吗？今年会开花吗？
还是突来的霜冻惊扰了它的温床？b
哦，把大犬弄远点，那是人的朋友，11
75 不然它会用爪子把尸体再挖出来！
你！虚伪的读者！——我的同流——我的兄弟！"12

## 二、棋局

她坐的椅子，像锃亮的御座，13
在大理石地面熠熠生辉，镜子
支在镂着果实藤蔓的框柱中
80 藤蔓中有个金色丘比特向外探望
（另一个把眼睛藏在翅膀后面）
将七枝烛台的火苗翻倍
又把烛光反射到桌面，而
她那珠宝的晶晶华光从富丽的
85 锦盒中升起，与烛光交相辉映；
一个个象牙瓶和彩色玻璃瓶
瓶盖开启，她那些合成香精，

---

合但丁笔下的地狱，那里可以遇见亡魂。承接上文死亡的钟声将人带入地狱一样"诡异"的地方。
a "尸体"的原文"corpse"，另指巨花魔芋，俗称尸花。
b "突来的霜冻惊扰了它的温床"：这里一语三关，包含了苗、性和死。

荒原

膏状，粉状，液态——怪味暗飘
迷乱并淹没着嗅觉；窗口空气
90 清新袭来，一经搅动，气味上升，
把细长的烛焰挑得粗壮，
又把烛烟直甩到镶板顶棚间，[14]
拂动着方格天花板上的图案。
浸了铜盐的巨块海漂木[a]
95 燃出绿色和橙色，色彩映在石框上，
那悲伤的火光中，游着一头雕刻的海豚。
古旧的壁炉台上展示着
犹如窗口展示着田野风光[15]
一幅菲洛墨拉的变形，她被野蛮的国王[16]
100 所强暴；然而那夜莺却[17]
用她凛然的呼声填满整个荒漠
她恒定地在呼喊，而世界至今在驱赶，
"啾啾"，对着肮脏的耳朵。
还有些时光的残桩旧事
105 陈述在墙壁上；各种形体凝视着
探出身，斜倚着，嘘静围起的空间。
脚步声在楼梯上嚓嚓作响。
火光下，发刷下，她的头发
散发开像飞溅的点点火星
110 闪作话语，接着是一片死寂。

---

[a] 海漂木经海水浸泡后留在上面的铜盐燃烧时呈绿色。

"今夜我神经很糟。是,很糟。留下陪我。
跟我说话。你为什么总不说话。说话呀。
你在想什么?想什么?什么?
我从来不知道你在想什么。想想吧。"

115 我想我们落到了鼠坑里,[18]
　　死人丢弃了尸骨的地方。[a]

　　"那是什么声音?"
　　　　　　是门底的风。[19]
　　"那又是什么声音?风在干什么?"
120　　　　　什么都没有什么都没干。
　　　　　　　　　　"那
　　你什么都不知道?什么都没看见?什么都
　　不记得吗?"

　　　　我记得
125 那些明珠原是他的眼睛。
　　"你是活着还是死了?你脑壳里啥也没有吗?"[20]
　　　　　　可是
　　哦哦哦哦那莎士比黑亚式的拉格——[b]

---

[a] 这里的意象可能来自一战中士兵抛尸于老鼠成灾的战壕,暗含失去雄风和精神,还暗喻两人的婚姻现状。
[b] 拉格:拉格泰姆,散拍音乐。这里指当年一首流行的拉格泰姆歌曲。艾略特在标题中用了"Shakespe*h*erian Rag"拼法,应是有意的。下面两行转引自曲中歌词"最为机智/非常雅致"。

9

多么雅致
130 多么机智
"这下我该怎么办呢？该干什么呢？"
"我就这个样子冲出去，浪荡街头ᵃ
披散着头发，像这样。明天又该怎么办？
我们到底还能干什么？"
135 　　　　　　　　十点钟供热水。
如果下雨，四点钟来一辆闭蓬车。
我们还要下一局棋，
撑着眼皮巴望那一声敲门。²¹

丽尔的丈夫退伍时，我说——
140 我毫不含糊，亲口对她说，
**赶紧着到点了**ᵇ
艾伯特要回来了，去把自己收拾利落点。
他一准想知道他给你做牙的钱
你都花到哪儿了。他给了，我在场的。
145 去把牙全拔了吧，丽尔，配一副像样的，
他说，真心说，我真没法看你。
我也没法看你，我说，想想可怜的艾伯特，
他当兵四年了，想好好快活一下，ᶜ

---

ᵃ 那个年代(1922)披散着头发行走街头是妓女形象。比较原文"walk the street"与短语"walk the streets"。
ᵇ 酒吧关门时服务生催客离去的习惯用语。
ᶜ 四年指第一次世界大战的四年（1914-1918）。

你要是不给他，有人会给的，我说。
150　哦，有么，她说。差不多吧，我说。
那我就知道该谢谁了，说着她直盯了我一眼。
**赶紧着到点了**
就算你不乐意，也将就些吧，我说。
别人能挑三拣四，你可没得挑。
155　要是艾伯特跑了，可别怪没人提醒你。
你也不嫌寒碜，我说，看着那么老相。
（她才三十一岁。）
有啥办法，她拉长了脸说，
都怪吃的那些药，打胎的，她说。
160　（她已经五次了，生小乔治差点送了命。）
药房说没事，可我再也不像从前了。
你真是个大傻瓜，我说。
可要是艾伯特不让你安生，就是这样，我说，
不想生孩子你干嘛要结婚？
165　**赶紧着到点了**
哦，那个星期天艾伯特在家，弄了条热熏腿
他们请我到家去吃饭，趁热品尝美味——
**赶紧着到点了**
**赶紧着到点了**
170　晚安，比尔。晚安，露。晚安，梅。晚安。[a]
拜拜。晚安。晚安。

---

[a] 注意原文 170-171 两行中"晚安"的拼法："Goonight"。

 荒原

晚安，太太们，晚安，可爱的小姐们，晚安，晚安。a

## 三、火诫b

河的蓬帐已破：树叶的残指
抓了抓便沉入湿湿的河堤。风
175 掠过褐色大地，没人听见。美少女都已离去。
可爱的泰晤士河啊，你轻轻地流，等我唱完我的歌。22
河面不再漂浮着空瓶子、三明治纸、
丝手绢、硬纸盒、烟蒂头
也没了夏夜的其他痕迹。美少女都已离去。
180 还有她们的朋友，城中大亨们的浪荡后人；
都已经离去，没有留下地址。
坐在莱蒙湖的水边，我哭了……c
可爱的泰晤士河啊，你轻轻地流，等我唱完我的歌，
可爱的泰晤士河啊，你轻轻地流，我话声不高语不多。

---

a 典出《哈姆雷特》第四幕第五场中奥菲莉亚临死前的告别："晚安，太太们；晚安，可爱的小姐们；晚安，晚安！"另，奥菲莉亚精神失常后手持花束溺亡，极可能与本诗中手持风信子的女孩和溺亡的腓尼基水手相暗合。
b 佛陀在《火诫》中劝告人们摈弃各种欲望之火，以期脱离轮回，达到涅槃。
c 莱蒙湖（Leman）是瑞士洛桑人对日内瓦湖的称呼。艾略特在洛桑治病期间完成此诗的一部分。许多人认为这一行暗合《圣经·诗篇137》："坐在巴比伦的河边，我们哭了。"英文词"leman"旧指情妇。

185　可是我听见在背后的寒风中ᵃ
　　白骨咔咔作响，咧笑咯咯出声。


　　一只老鼠轻轻穿过草丛
　　拖着黏湿的肚皮在岸上爬行
　　而那个冬日的傍晚，我正在
190　煤气厂背后呆滞的渠中垂钓
　　默想着我那兄王的海难
　　以及之前我父王的惨死。²³
　　白尸裸露在低洼的湿地
　　遗骨散落在矮燥的阁楼，
195　只是被老鼠踢得作响，年复一年。
　　可是在背后我不时听见²⁴
　　喇叭和马达的声响，春天这声响²⁵
　　将送斯维尼到波特太太身旁。ᵇ
　　哦，月光闪闪把波特太太照²⁶
200　也把她的女儿照
　　她俩用苏打水洗双脚
　　哦那些童声，在穹顶中歌唱！²⁷


　　咕，咕，咕

---

ᵃ 见原注 196 行。
ᵇ 斯维尼是艾略特创造的粗野人物，出现在他的多首诗中；波特太太是开罗一家妓院的老鸨。她们母女被一战中的澳大利亚士兵编入拉格泰姆歌词里，下面三行即来自歌词，其猥亵程度已被艾略特弱化。

 荒原

啾啾，啾啾，啾啾ª
205 那样粗野地强暴。
忒鲁ᵇ

诡异的城啊
在冬日正午的褐色雾中，
尤金尼德斯先生，那位士麦那商人
210 胡子拉碴，满满一口袋葡萄干28
伦敦到岸价：见票即付，
操一口粗俗的法语邀请我
到坎农街酒店进午餐
随后到大都会度周末。ᶜ

215 那紫色黄昏时分，当眼和腰
从桌面抬起，当人型机器在等候
像出租车搏动着等候的时分，
我提瑞舍斯，瞎着眼，搏动在两性间，29
长着皱巴巴女人乳房的老汉，却能看到

---

ª 参看约翰·利利（John Lyly）剧作《坎帕斯佩》（*Campaspe*）中的歌："什么鸟儿这样唱，然而又是这样哭？哦，是那被强暴的夜莺。啾啾，啾啾，忒鲁，她哭道"。
ᵇ 忒鲁：既是本诗 99 行中强奸了菲洛墨拉的色雷斯国王名字忒鲁斯（Tereus）的呼格 Tereu，也是伊丽莎白时期诗歌中夜莺所唱的歌里惯用的词，见上注，在英文中与 to rue 谐音。二者皆含谴责之意。
ᶜ 大都会：英国海边度假胜地布莱顿的一家豪华连锁酒店，邀请到这里度周末有性暧昧意味。

| | |
|---|---|
| 220 | 那紫色黄昏时分,傍晚归家的时段, |
| | 招呼水手离海回家的时段,30 |
| | 打字员茶点时间回家,清理早餐, |
| | 点着炉火,摆出食品罐罐。 |
| | 窗外,领受着最后的阳光 |
| 225 | 岌岌可危地晾着她的连裤衣 |
| | 沙发上堆着(夜里当作床) |
| | 长筒袜、拖鞋、背心和胸衣。 |
| | 我提瑞舍斯,长着干巴奶子的老汉 |
| | 觉察到这一幕,就预言了下文—— |
| 230 | 我也在等候那位预期的客人。 |
| | 他来了,那个年轻轻的粉刺脸, |
| | 房产经纪的小职员,眼神颇为轻佻, |
| | 这个低微之人身上摆着的自信 |
| | 宛若布雷德福暴发户头上的丝礼帽。[a] |
| 235 | 此刻时机很有利,据他猜测, |
| | 饭已吃完但见她,无聊困乏, |
| | 探手探脚拉过来搂抱亲热, |
| | 虽未见她来相迎也没遭骂。 |
| | 脸一红来心一横立刻进攻; |
| 240 | 上下其手去摸索没遇抗拒; |
| | 他那虚荣不需要任何回应, |
| | 一厢情愿把冷漠当成乐意。 |

---

[a] 布雷德福是英国约克郡的一个产业城,其羊毛业和纺织业一战期间造就了一批暴发户。

（而我提瑞舍斯，早已领受过
这沙发这床榻上演的所有；
245 我曾经在底比斯城墙下坐，ᵃ
也曾在最卑微的死人中走。）ᵇ
他再把那最后一吻施舍上，
便摸着去路，只见楼梯没照亮……

她转身对着镜子看了看，
250 把那离去的情人全忘掉；
大脑中半个念头忽一闪：
"既然已经完事：完事就好。"
当可爱的女人失足犯傻，31
再次独自在家踱步之际，
255 她机械地抬手抹平头发，
又放了张唱片给留声机。

"这音乐贴着水面掠过我身边"32
穿过河岸街，沿维多利亚女王街直上。
伦敦城啊伦敦城，我时而能听见。ᶜ
260 泰晤士下街的一家酒肆旁，

---

ᵃ 在索福克勒斯的悲剧《俄狄浦斯王》中，正是提瑞舍斯在底比斯城墙下的披露，让俄狄浦斯王得知自己未能逃脱杀父娶母的不幸命运。
ᵇ 提瑞舍斯虽然得享长寿，但终有一死，而他死后仍有知觉。荷马史诗《奥德赛》中，奥德修斯造访冥间时曾与他相遇。
ᶜ "伦敦城"即 The City，指伦敦金融区。

一只曼陀林那悦耳的哀鸣
还有里面叽叽嘎嘎的语声
午间渔贩们在那里歇晌：那里
马格纳斯殉道堂的墙上[33]
265 是爱奥尼亚式白底描金的莫名辉煌。

    河面上渗出[34]
    油花和沥青
    画舫只只
    随着退潮漂荡
270     红帆
    大张
    顺着风，摇摆在沉重的桅杆上。
    画舫浪拍
    漂移的原木
275     流过多格斯岛
    直下格林尼治水域。
        喂呵啦啦  咧呀 [a]
        哇啦啦  咧呀啦啦

    伊丽莎白和莱斯特[35]

---

[a] 这"啦啦"歌让人联想到瓦格纳《尼伯龙根的指环》（*Der Ring des Nibelungen*）系列中四部歌剧的第一部《莱茵的黄金》（*Das Rheingold*）和第四部《诸神的黄昏》（*Götterdämmerung*）中莱茵河女儿所唱的歌。她们唱了两遍副歌"喂呵啦啦　咧呀 哇啦啦　咧呀啦啦"，一遍"啦啦"。

280　　击水的船桨
　　　船尾的形状
　　　像镀金的贝壳
　　　红色间着金黄
　　　轻快的水波
285　　在两岸拍成细浪
　　　西南风
　　　带向下游
　　　响亮的钟声
　　　白色的塔楼
290　　　　喂呵啦啦　　咧呀
　　　　　哇啦啦　咧呀啦啦


　　　"来往的电车灰土土的树。
　　　海布里生我。里士满和基尤[36a]
　　　毁我。到了里士满我抬起双膝
295　　仰卧船板在窄窄的独木舟。"


　　　"我双脚踩在穆尔埃，心[b]
　　　却踩在我脚底。事情过后
　　　他哭了。他许诺要'自新'。
　　　我没说话。我能有啥怨和仇？"

---

[a] 海布里、里士满、基尤都是伦敦市郊住宅区。
[b] 穆尔埃：伦敦东区的贫民区。

300   "在马盖特的沙滩上。ᵃ
      我头脑空空
      什么联想都没有。
      破裂的指甲满手的脏。ᵇ
      我们这些卑微之人
305   无所求。"
                  啦啦

      于是我来到迦太基³⁷

      烧呀烧呀烧呀烧呀³⁸
      主啊,您救我出来吧³⁹
310   主啊,您救啊

      烧呀


# 四、溺亡ᶜ

腓尼基人弗莱巴,死了已经两星期,ᵈ

---

ᵃ 马盖特:英国东南滨海一处度假胜地,艾略特曾遵医嘱于1921年在此休养一个月。
ᵇ 从草稿上划掉的一行可以看出艾略特想象的脏手应是男人的手,即泰晤士女儿父兄之手。
ᶜ 埃兹拉·庞德让艾略特删掉了《溺亡》的前82行,其文字描述一个水手航海遇难的历程。
ᵈ 这一段文字来自艾略特1918年所作法文诗《在餐馆》,两处大同小异。法文原作试译如下:"腓尼基人弗莱巴,溺亡

荒原

忘掉了鸥鸟的鸣叫,深海的浪涌
也忘掉了盈利和亏损。

315　　　　　海底一股暗流
悄声剔净他的骨头。一浮一沉中
他穿过一生每个阶段穿过青春
陷入漩涡。

　　　　　无论是不是犹太人
320　哦,你这位转动舵轮查看风向的,
想想弗莱巴,他曾和你一样高大英俊。

## 五、雷之语[40]

火炬映红汗淋淋的脸庞过后[a]
果园那寒霜般的寂静过后[b]
乱石之间历经的磨难
325　监牢宫殿中的

---

"已经十五天,/忘了鸥鸟的叫声,忘了康沃尔海的浪涌/也忘了盈利和亏损和一货舱罐头;/一股洋流载他去远方,/把他带到前世的各个阶段。/试想吧,这么悲惨的命运;/然而,他也曾高大英俊。"

[a] 参见《圣经·约翰福音》第18章第3节:"犹大领了一队兵,以及祭司长和法利赛人的圣殿警卫,拿着灯笼、火把和兵器来到园里。"

[b] 暗指客西马尼园,耶路撒冷的一个果园。按照新约圣经和基督教传统说法,耶稣被钉死在十字架上的前夜,和他的门徒在最后的晚餐之后前往此处祷告。从322行到328行指的是耶稣从被捕到受难的整个过程。

哭叫呼喊还有远山
春雷的回响都过去之后
那位曾经活着的已经死去
我们曾经活着的正在死去
330 只在耐心等候

这里没有水只有烂石头
只有石头没有水只有沙土路
土路头顶绕，绕在大山里
山是石头山，山间没有水
335 要是能有水咱就停步把水喝
身处烂石间不能停步或思索
汗水已流干双脚陷沙土
多么渴望石头之间能有水
死山嘴里是龋齿滴水不会吐
340 不能站来不能躺坐也坐不住
这山里就连安静也没有
只会干打瘆雷不下雨
这山里就连孤独也没有
只有阴沉的赤脸在讥吼
345 发自泥裂破屋的门口
　　　　　但愿能有水
　　没有烂石头
　　就算有石头
　　但愿也有水

　　　　也有水
350　　有泉水
　　　　石头之间一汪水
　　　　哪怕只是一缕水声
　　　　不是知了
　　　　和枯草在歌唱
355　　而是石头上的流水声
　　　　和松树上隐居鸫的歌声
　　　　滴答滴答答答答[41]
　　　　可就是没有水

　　　　那第三个人是谁，他总在你身边走？
360　　我点人数时，只有你我在一起[42]
　　　　可当我抬头看前方那白色的路
　　　　总是另有一个人在你身边走
　　　　悄悄滑行裹着棕色斗篷，罩着头
　　　　我不知道那是男人还是女人
365　　——可那是谁呀他在你的另一头？

　　　　那是什么声音凄厉在空中[43]
　　　　可是慈母哀伤的喃喃声
　　　　那群罩着头的是什么人，蜂拥
　　　　在无尽的原野，跌撞在坼裂的大地
370　　只有扁扁的地平线才是边缘
　　　　那是哪座城市在山的那边

崩裂、重建、爆炸在紫色暮空
城楼倒坍中
亚力山大　雅典　耶路撒冷
375　维也纳　伦敦
诡异啊

一个女人绷紧她那黑色长发
在那些琴弦上弄出嚓嚓音响
婴儿脸的蝙蝠在紫色暮光下
380　发出呼啸，扇动着翅膀
头朝下沿着污黑的墙壁爬行
几座钟塔倒挂在空中
鸣响着勾起怀想的报时钟声
还有吟唱之声传出空池和枯井。a

385　在这群山环抱的残破山沟
教堂四周那坍塌的坟墓上
幽暗的月光下，荒草在歌唱
那空空的教堂，只是风的家。b
没有窗户，门在摇晃，
390　枯骨无以为害。
只有一只雄鸡站在屋脊上

---

a 《旧约》中"池"和"井"是信仰的活水之源，这里空池和枯井则象征信仰的干涸。
b 指寻求圣杯的骑士来到凶险教堂前一无所见、只见荒芜的绝望一刻。空幻是对骑士的最后考验。

 荒原

咯咯里咯，咯咯里咯ᵃ
随着雷电一闪。接着一股湿风
带来了雨

395　恒河干瘪了，萎靡的树叶ᵇ
　　等待着雨，而滚滚乌云
　　远远地聚集在喜马望山。ᶜ
　　莽林猫腰蹲伏着，静默无声。
　　于是雷发话了
400　哒
　　哒塔：我们施予了什么？⁴⁴
　　朋友啊，热血激荡着我的心
　　那顷刻间舍弃的非凡勇气
　　那一世审慎也无法撤回的勇气
405　借此，唯独借此，我们得以生存
　　那勇气，它不会在我们的讣告中
　　不会在蜘蛛善意覆盖的墓志铭里⁴⁵
　　也不会在瘦律师在我们那空屋
　　所拆开的封条下

---

ᵃ 原文为法文："Co co rico co co rico"。公鸡叫声在法国也是胜利和自豪之声；这里表示恶魔将离去。这两行被认为暗指《圣经·路加福音》第22章第62节耶稣对彼得所说的话："今日鸡叫以先，你要三次不认我。"
ᵇ 恒河：诗人用了人格化的"Ganga"一词，即印度教中的恒河女神。
ᶜ 喜马望山（Himavant）：人格化的喜马拉雅山脉，即印度教中的雪山神，是恒河女神之父。参照前注。

410 哒

　　哒亚德万：我听见那钥匙⁴⁶

　　在门上转动了一次，只一次

　　我们想到钥匙，各自在牢房

　　每人想到钥匙，各自确认牢房

415 只有在黄昏，缥缈的传说才能

　　让垮掉的科里奥兰纳斯复活片刻ª

　　哒

　　哒密阿塔：船儿愉快地回应

　　那撑帆划桨的行家里手

420 大海平静，你的心，受到邀请，

　　也会愉快地回应，随着自制之手

　　顺从地跳动ᵇ


　　　　　我坐在岸上

　　垂钓，背后是一片干燥的原野⁴⁷

425 我是否至少该把自己的家园整理好？ᶜ

---

ª 科里奥兰纳斯（Coriolanus）：莎士比亚以其名为题所作历史悲剧的人物，公元前5世纪罗马大将，出于狂傲，两次背叛而败亡。这里借他之名描写人陷于自己的精神牢房，只有在夜间借助天启忘掉自我，才能复活片刻。

ᵇ 指内心的自制会令生命历程一帆风顺。

ᶜ 典出《圣经·以赛亚书》第38章第1节："耶和华这样说，你要把你的家整顿妥当，因为你快要死去，不能存活。"

 荒原

伦敦桥要垮掉了垮掉了垮掉了[a]
他随即隐没在那炼化之火中[48]
何时我才能像燕子一般——哦,燕子,燕子[49]
那阿基坦王子在毁弃的塔楼中[50]
430  我用了这些散片支撑我的废墟
好吧,我就遵你所嘱。希罗尼莫又疯了。[51]
哒塔。哒亚德万。哒密阿塔。

  玄静  玄静  玄静[52]

---

[a] 著名儿歌《伦敦桥要垮掉了》里面还有一句"拿一把钥匙锁起她"。

# 作者原注

1 这首诗,不仅标题,甚至构思以及随之而来的大部分象征手法,都来自杰西·L.韦斯顿小姐有关圣杯传说的著作《从祭仪到传奇》(麦克米兰版)一书的启发。我从其中借鉴之多,可以说韦斯顿小姐的著作远比我自己的注释更能解答诗中的疑难之处;因而无论谁认为值得寻求解答,我都向他推荐这本书(且不说此书本身就引人入胜)。总的说我还受益于深深影响了我们这一代人的另一部人类学著作;我指的是《金枝》;而主要用到的是《阿多尼斯、阿提斯、奥西里斯》两卷。熟悉这两部著作的人都会立即认出诗中提及的一些有关繁衍生长的仪式。

## 一、葬亡

2 第20行。参阅《以西结书》第二章第一节。
【译者按:艾略特指的是《圣经·旧约·以西结书》中"他对我说:人子啊,你站起来,我要和你说话。"】

3 23。参阅《传道书》第十二章第五节。
【译者按:诗人指的是《圣经·旧约·传道书》中警示老年凄惶的一段:"人怕高处,路上有惊慌;杏树开花,蚱蜢成为重担,欲望不再挑起;因为人归他永远的家,吊丧的在街上往来。"】

4 31。见《特里斯坦与伊索尔德》第一幕第 5—8 行。
【译者按：德国音乐家瓦格纳歌剧《特里斯坦与伊索尔德》描写特里斯坦骑士与伊索尔德的爱情悲剧。伊索尔德被用船带到康沃尔与特里斯坦的叔叔马克王成婚，这是她在船上听到一名水手思念女友时唱的歌。】

5 42。同上，第三幕第 24 行。
【译者按：原文是濒死的特里斯坦在等待伊索尔德时，帮他瞭望大海的牧羊人告诉他的话。】

6 46。我并不熟悉塔罗纸牌的确切构成，我与之有所偏离显然是出于为我所用的目的。这套纸牌传统构成中那张倒悬者之所以合我所用是由于以下两点：我在心里把他同弗雷泽（译者按：即上述《金枝》的作者）的倒悬的神相联系，也同第五节中去以马忤斯的罩着头的使徒相联系。腓尼基水手和商人稍后出现；而"成群的人"和"溺亡"放在第四节处理。至于"持三根权杖的人"（塔罗牌中实有的一张），我则自作主张地把他跟渔王联系在一起。

7 60。参见波德莱尔：

"人群涌动的城，充满迷梦的城，
　那里幽灵在光天化日下搭讪过路的人。"

【译者按：原文出自波德莱尔诗集《恶之花》中的一首诗《七个老头子》（*Les Sept Viellards*）。中文为译者提供。】

8 63。参见《地狱篇》第三章第 55—57 行：

> "一大群人
> 排成长龙，我简直不敢相信，
> 死神竟毁掉这么多人的生命。"

【译者按：《神曲·地狱篇》中但丁在冥间见到一大群人在巨痛中呻吟时发出的惊叹。本书所引但丁《神曲》中文皆摘自黄文捷译本。】

9　64。参看《神曲·地狱篇》第四章第 25-27 行：

> "这里，从送入耳际的声音来看，
> 没有别的，只有长吁短叹，
> 这叹声使流动在这永劫之地的空气也不住抖颤。"

10　68。这是我时常注意到的情景。

11　74。参看韦伯斯特《白魔》中的挽歌。

【译者按：艾略特指的是第五幕第四场中"哦，把那狼弄远点，那是人类的敌人"。诗中"the Dog"则指天狼星/犬星 Sirius。】

12　76。见波德莱尔《恶之花》前言。

## 二、棋局

13　77。参见《安东尼与克莉奥佩特拉》第二幕第二场第 190 行。

【译者按：艾略特指莎士比亚该剧中的描述："她乘坐的画舫，像锃亮的御座/闪耀在水面上"。】

14 92。镶板顶棚。见维吉尔《埃涅阿斯纪》第一部第726行：

> 燃烧的灯挂在镶板顶棚上，
> 火把的烈焰驱走了黑夜。

【译者按：转译自 T.C. William 的英译: "from the gilded vault/far-blazing cressets swing, or torches bright/drive the dark night away"，描写的是迦太基女王狄多举办盛宴招待埃涅阿斯的场景。狄多爱上埃涅阿斯，后为爱而死。】

15 98。田野风光。见弥尔顿《失乐园》第四卷第140行。

【译者按：艾略特指的是撒旦进入伊甸园时看到的田野风光，之后他诱惑了夏娃及亚当，致他们被贬入苦难世界，难免一死。】

16 99。见奥维德《变形记》第六卷菲洛墨拉。

【译者按：希腊神话，菲洛墨拉是雅典公主，被姐夫色雷斯国王忒鲁斯强奸后悲愤而变成夜莺。】

17 100。见本诗第三节第 204 行。

18 115。见本诗第三节第 195 行。

19 118。参见韦伯斯特："风还在门边吹么？"

【译者按：指韦伯斯特戏剧《魔鬼的诉讼案》(*The Devil's Law Case*) 第三幕第二场中一位外科医生的问话。】

20 126。见本诗第一节第 37 和 48 行。

【译者按：应该是指此二处所涉及到的死亡主题。】

21 138。参见米德尔顿剧《女人谨防女人》中的棋局。

【译者按：指托马斯·米德尔顿（Thomas Middleton）在 Women beware Women 剧中所描述的棋局，局中每一招棋都与另一间屋子里佛罗伦萨公爵实施诱奸的步骤相对应。】

## 三、火诫

22 176。参看斯宾塞《婚礼歌》。

【译者按：指其中每一段结尾处的叠句，试译如下："在此新婚之日，这短暂一刻：/可爱的泰晤士河啊，你轻轻地流，等我唱完我的歌。"诗人在此反其意而化用之。】

23 192。参见《暴风雨》第一幕第二场。

【译者按：指莎士比亚剧中斐迪南的台词，试译如下："当我坐在岸上，再次哭悼我那父王的海难，这音乐贴着水面掠过我身边。"】

24 196。参见安德鲁·马维尔《致他的忸怩女友》。

【译者按：艾略特指的是 To His Coy Mistress 中诗句"可是在我背后总能听见/时间战车插翅逼近眼前。"见附录所载译者译文。】

25 197。参见约翰·戴《蜜蜂议会》：

　　"只要侧耳聆听，你会忽然听见
　　喇叭和打猎的声响，春天这声响
　　会把阿克泰恩送到戴安娜的身旁，
　　在那大家都能看到她赤裸的肌肤……"【译者自译】

26　199。这几行词摘自一首民谣，我并不知道这首民谣的出处：我是在澳大利亚悉尼间接听来的。

27　202。见魏尔伦著《帕西法尔》。

【译者按：《帕西法尔》中有句："Et O ces voix d'enfants, chantant dans la coupole！"】

28　210。葡萄干报价为"伦敦到岸价免运费保险费"；提单等文件在收到即期汇票时交付买方。

29　218。提瑞舍斯虽然只是个旁观者而算不上"人物"，却是这首诗中最重要的角色，他串起了所有其他人物。就像独眼商人和葡萄干推销者可以融合为腓尼基水手，而后者与那不勒斯王子斐迪南也不能完全分开一样，所有的女人也都是同一个女人，而男女两种性别则在提瑞舍斯身上合为一体。提瑞舍斯所"见到"的，其实正是诗的实质内容。奥维德写的整个这一段富有人类学意义：

> ……他们说，朱庇特很快乐
> （酒后）感觉很兴奋，忘掉了
> 拘束和謹慎，于是消磨着时间
> 和朱诺开玩笑。"我认为，"他对她说
> "你们女人从做爱中能得到更多快乐
> 比起我们可怜的男人。"她不同意，
> 所以两人决定把这个问题交给
> 见多识广的提瑞舍斯评判：他了解
> 做爱时男女两方面的感觉。
> 有一次他遇到了两条蛇在交配
> 在绿色的树林里，就把它们打散了，

于是，他从男人变成了女人，
做了七年女人后，又一次看到
这两条蛇交配，又一次把它们打
散了，一边说："如果有这样的魔法
给你一击，男人就能变成女人，
或许女人也能变成男人。值得一试。"
于是他又变成了男人；作为裁判，
他站在朱庇特一边。而朱诺
是个输不起的人，她说裁判
总是闭着眼，就把他变成永远如此。
一个神不能推翻另一个神的行为，
但全能的天父出于怜悯，
作为补偿，赋予了提瑞舍斯
预知未来的能力，获得一些
荣耀以减轻他所受的惩罚。

【译者按：这段诗系译者根据罗尔夫·汉弗莱斯（Rolphe Humphries）英译奥维德《变形记：提瑞舍斯的故事》第三卷第318-343行转译。】

30 221。这一行与萨福的原诗句也许并不完全一样，不过我想的是"海边"或"小渔船"渔夫傍晚回家的情景。

31 253。参照哥尔德史密斯（Goldsmith）《威克菲尔德的牧师》中的歌。

【译者按：指第二十四章中奥莉维亚回到自己被诱奸之地时所唱的歌，见附录所载译者译文。】

32 257。见《暴风雨》，同上。

【译者按：指原注 192 行。】

33 264。我认为马格纳斯殉道堂的室内设计是雷恩最精美的室内建筑作品之一。见《建议拆除的十九座市内教堂》（P. S. King & Son, Ltd.）。

【译者按：克里斯托佛·雷恩，著名建筑师。】

34 266。泰晤士河（3 位）女儿的歌开始于此。从 292 行到 306 行她们轮流发话。参见《诸神的黄昏》第三幕第一场：莱茵河女儿。

【译者按：《诸神的黄昏》（Götterdämmerung）是瓦格纳的四部系列歌剧作品《尼伯龙根的指环》之第四部。】

35 279。见弗劳德著《伊丽莎白》第一卷第四章，德夸德拉致西班牙国王菲利普的信：

"下午我们乘着画舫在河上观看赛事。她（女王）单独与罗伯特伯爵还有我自己在船尾甲板上，这时他们说话开始不着边际起来，甚至到头来罗伯特伯爵还说，既然我就在场，只要女王乐意，他们俩当即成婚也无不可。"

【译者按：詹姆士·安东尼·弗劳德是英国历史学家；阿尔瓦雷斯·德夸德拉是西班牙一位主教兼驻英大使。罗伯特即罗伯特·达德利，第一代莱斯特伯爵，英国女王伊丽莎白一世的宠臣。传闻二人一向亲密，但也可能只是政治同谋而已。】

36 293。参阅《炼狱篇》第五首第 133 行：

"请记住我,我就是那个皮娅,
锡耶纳养育了我,而马雷马却把我毁掉。"

【译者按:这些是《神曲·炼狱篇》中锡耶纳的托洛梅伊在炼狱遇到但丁时说的话,讲述她生在锡耶纳,又在马雷马被丈夫所谋杀之事。】

37 307。见圣奥古斯丁的《忏悔录》:

"于是我来到了迦太基,这里形形色色
骚动的邪爱唱响在我耳旁。"

38 308。这些词语引自佛陀的火戒(其重要性相当于耶稣的山上宝训)。全文可见已故亨利·克拉克·沃伦的《佛教英译》(*Buddhism in Translation*)(哈佛东方丛书)。沃伦先生是西方佛学研究的伟大先驱之一。

【译者按:赵萝蕤先生在其译者按中所译的火戒这一段非常优美,可供参考,此不另译。大意是一切感官,一切欲望都在燃烧,信众应善加克服,以期解脱。】

39 309。仍见于圣奥古斯丁的《忏悔录》。苦修主义在东方与西方的这两个代表能并列一处,成为本诗这一部分的完结,并非偶然。

## 五、雷之语

40 第五节第一部分有三个主题:去往以马忤斯、走近凶险教堂(见韦斯顿小姐的著作)、东欧今日的衰微。

41 357。这是我在魁北克省听到过的隐夜鸫(Turdus aonalaschkae pallasii)。查普曼说(《北美东部鸟类手册》）"这种鸟最喜僻静的林木丛……它的叫声不很多样，音量也不大，而其声调的纯净甜美和精致婉转则是无与伦比的。"它那"滴水歌声"名不虚传。

[42] 360。下面这几行是受到一篇南极探险纪行（我忘记是哪篇了，可能是沙克尔顿（Shackleton）的那篇）激发所得。据说探险队员们精疲力竭之时，一直有个错觉，好像比清点到的人数还多出一人。

[43] 366-376。参见赫尔曼·黑塞《混沌一瞥》：

"半个欧洲，至少半个东欧，已经在走向混乱，怀着神圣的妄想醉醺醺地沿着深渊挪动，同时也在歌唱，像德米特里·卡拉马索夫（Dmitri Karamasoff）那样醉醺醺地唱着颂歌。受到冒犯的布尔乔亚听到发出嘲笑，圣人和先知听到则泪流不已。"

[44] 401。"Datta, dayadhvam, dāmyata"（施舍、仁慈、自制）。关于雷声意义的寓言见于《大森林奥义书》（*Brihadaranyaka--Upanishad*）第五卷第一章。译文见保罗·雅各布·德森（Deussen）的《吠陀的六十篇奥义书》（*Sechzig Upanishads des Veda*）第489页。

【译者按：《大森林奥义书》中的这一段，此处借用黄宝生先生的中文译本如下：

生主的三支后裔天神、凡人和阿修罗曾经作为梵行者，住在父亲生主那里。梵行期满后，天神们说道："请您给我们指示。"于是，生主对他们说了一个音节："Da。"然后，问道："你们理解吗？"他们回答说:"我们理解。您对我们说:'你们要自制(dāmyata)!'"生主说道:"唵,你们已经理解。"

注:"梵行者"指学生。按照婆罗门教,人生的第一阶段是梵行期,即拜师求学。

然后,凡人们对生主说道:"请您给我们指示。"生主对他们说了一个音节:"Da。"然后,问道:"你们理解吗?"他们回答说:"我们理解。您对我们说:'你们要施舍(datta)!'"生主说道:"唵,你们已经理解。"

然后,阿修罗们对生主说道:"请您给我们指示。"生主对他们说了一个音节:"Da。"然后,问道:"你们理解吗?"他们回答说:"我们理解。您对我们说:'你们要仁慈(dayadhvam)!'"生主说道:"唵,你们已经理解。"

作为天国之声的雷鸣回响着:"Da,Da,Da!"也就是"你们要自制!你们要施舍!你们要仁慈!因此,应该学会这三者:自制、施舍和仁慈。】

45 407。参见韦伯斯特《白魔》第五幕第六场:

"她们又将改嫁
不等蛆虫蛀穿你的裹尸布,不等蜘蛛
为你的墓志铭织起薄幕。"

46 411。参见《炼狱篇》第三十三首第46行:

> "我听到可怕塔楼的下层，
> 传来钉门的声音。"

又见 F.H.布拉德雷《表象与实在》第 346 页：

> "我的外在感觉跟我的思想感情一样，都是只属于我个人的。在这两方面，我的经历都落在我个人的圈子内，对外是封闭的；每一个领域中的所有因素都一样，都与周围的领域相隔绝。简而言之，整个世界，如果看作是显现给某灵魂的存在，它对那个灵魂就是独特的、私密的。"

【译者按：《神曲·炼狱篇》中的引文是乌格里诺（Ugolino della Gherardesca）回忆起他同他的两个儿子两个孙子被锁在塔楼中，活活饿死时所说。他听到钥匙只转一圈是因为狱吏锁门后就将钥匙扔进河里。他是因为背叛（科里奥兰纳斯也背着背叛之名）而被囚。另外，艾略特在哈佛大学的博士论文题为《F.H.布拉德利的哲学中的知识与经验》。】

47 424。见韦斯顿《从祭仪到传奇》中有关渔王的一章。
【译者按：韦斯顿在有关渔王的一章讨论了作为普世生命象征的鱼，有着古老的历史。它与创造生命保护生命的神相通。】

48 427。见《炼狱篇》第二十六首第 148 行：

> "'我现在请求您，看在那神力的份上
> ——它正在引导您走向那山梯的顶峰，

您能及时记得我的悲痛！'

他随即隐没在那冶炼他的烈火之中。"

49　428。见《维纳斯的守夜》。参照第二、三节中的菲洛墨拉。

【译者按："何时我才能像燕子一般"原文为拉丁文："Quando fiam uti chelidon"，来自佚名作品《维纳斯的守夜》（*Pervigilium Veneris*），作品中有句"她在唱，而我哑然。我的春天何时来？/何时我才能像燕子一般，不再无声？""哦，燕子，燕子"应是出自丁尼生的长篇叙事诗《公主》，其中有句："哦，燕子，燕子，飞啊，向南飞。"】

50　429。见热拉尔·德·内瓦尔的十四行诗《苦难的人》。

【译者按：热拉尔·德·内瓦尔（Gerard de Nerval）是法国诗人热拉尔·拉布吕尼（Gérard Labrunie）的笔名。其代表作十四行诗《苦难的人》（*El Desdichado*）开篇，试译如下：

我就是那阴暗者，——那鳏居者，——那悲极之人，
那阿基坦王子在毁弃的塔楼上：
我的孤星已死，——而我那缀星的琴
承载着忧伤郁结的黑色太阳。

原文为法文：

Je suis le Ténébreux, - le Veuf, - l'Inconsolé,
Le Prince d'Aquitaine à la Tour abolie:
Ma seule Etoile est morte, - et mon luth constellé
Porte le Soleil noir de la Mélancolie.】

[51] 431。见基德《西班牙悲剧》。

【译者按：即托马斯·基德（Thomas Kyd）所著 *Spanish Tragedy*。基德该剧是后来莎士比亚悲剧《哈姆雷特》的早期先导之一。希罗尼莫由于儿子霍拉肖遭嫉被害而发疯。意欲复仇，正不知所措，却被仇人邀请写一部剧以为宫廷娱乐。他便答应了，说"Why then *Ile fit you*"（古英文"我就遵你所嘱"），于是把儿子被害的故事和人物写进剧中，并请仇人参演剧中角色，趁机杀死谋害儿子的凶手。希罗尼莫的剧中剧也是悲剧，他写的剧中关键人物也都要死掉。希罗尼莫该剧以多种语言结尾，艾略特此诗承袭了这一手法。】

[52] 433。玄静（Shantih），如此重复，为《奥义书》的正规结语。"超越人所能理解的平安"略可译之。

【译者按：艾略特所引之句来自《圣经·新约·腓立比书》第四章第七节："神所赐那超越人所能了解的平安，必在基督耶稣里，保守你们的心怀意念。"】

（译自 T.S.艾略特 *The Waste Land* Boni&Liveright 1922）

# The Waste Land

### BY T. S. ELIOT

"Nam Sibyllam quidem Cumis ego ipse oculis meis vidi in ampulla pendere, et cum illi pueri dicerent: Σιβνλλατιθελειζ; repondebat illa: αποθαν ειν θελω."

For Ezra Pound
*il miglior fabbro.*

## I. The Burial of the Dead

April is the cruellest month, breeding
Lilacs out of the dead land, mixing
Memory and desire, stirring
Dull roots with spring rain.
5   Winter kept us warm, covering
Earth in forgetful snow, feeding
A little life with dried tubers.
Summer surprised us, coming over the Starnbergersee
With a shower of rain; we stopped in the colonnade,
10  And went on in sunlight, into the Hofgarten,
And drank coffee, and talked for an hour.

 荒原

    Bin gar keine Russin, stamm' aus Litauen, echt deutsch.
    And when we were children, staying at the archduke's,
    My cousin's, he took me out on a sled,
15  And I was frightened. He said, Marie,
    Marie, hold on tight. And down we went.
    In the mountains, there you feel free.
    I read, much of the night, and go south in the winter.

    What are the roots that clutch, what branches grow
20  Out of this stony rubbish? Son of man,
    You cannot say, or guess, for you know only
    A heap of broken images, where the sun beats,
    And the dead tree gives no shelter, the cricket no relief,
    And the dry stone no sound of water. Only
25  There is shadow under this red rock,
    (Come in under the shadow of this red rock),
    And I will show you something different from either
    Your shadow at morning striding behind you
    Or your shadow at evening rising to meet you;
30  I will show you fear in a handful of dust.

        *Frish weht der Wind*
        *Der Heimat zu*
        *Mein Irisch Kind,*
        *Wo weilest du?*

35  "You gave me hyacinths first a year ago;
    They called me the hyacinth girl."

--Yet when we came back, late, from the Hyacinth garden,
Your arms full, and your hair wet, I could not
Speak, and my eyes failed, I was neither
40    Living nor dead, and I knew nothing,
Looking into the heart of light, the silence.
*Oed' und leer das Meer.*

Madame Sosostris, famous clairvoyante,
Had a bad cold, nevertheless
45    Is known to be the wisest woman in Europe,
With a wicked pack of cards. Here, said she,
Is your card, the drowned Phoenician Sailor,
(Those are pearls that were his eyes. Look!)
Here is Belladonna, the Lady of the Rocks,
50    The lady of situations.
Here is the man with three staves, and here the Wheel,
And here is the one-eyed merchant, and this card,
Which is blank, is something he carries on his back,
Which I am forbidden to see. I do not find
55    The Hanged Man. Fear death by water.
I see crowds of people, walking round in a ring,
Thank you. If you see dear Mrs. Equitone,
Tell her I bring the horoscope myself:
One must be so careful these days.

60    Unreal City,
Under the brown fog of a winter dawn,
A crowd flowed over London Bridge, so many,

 荒原

I had not thought death had undone so many.
Sighs, short and infrequent, were exhaled,
65  And each man fixed his eyes before his feet.
Flowed up the hill and down King William Street,
To where Saint Mary Woolnoth kept the hours
With a dead sound on the final stroke of nine.
There I saw one I knew, and stopped him, crying: "Stetson!
70  "You who were with me in the ships at Mylae!
"That corpse you planted last year in your garden,
"Has it begun to sprout? Will it bloom this year?
"Or has the sudden frost disturbed its bed?
"O keep the Dog far hence, that's friend to men,
75  "Or with his nails he'll dig it up again!
"You! *Hypocrite lecteur!*---*mon semblable,--mon frere!*"


## II. A Game of Chess

The Chair she sat in, like a burnished throne,
Glowed on the marble, where the glass
Held up by standards wrought with fruited vines
80  From which a golden Cupidon peeped out
(Another hid his eyes behind his wing)
Doubled the flames of sevenbranched candelabra
Reflecting light upon the table as
The glitter of her jewels rose to meet it,
85  From satin cases poured in rich profusion.
In vials of ivory and colored glass

*The Waste Land*

Unstoppered, lurked her strange synthetic perfumes,
Unguent, powdered, or liquid--troubled, confused
And drowned the sense in odors; stirred by the air
90  That freshened from the window, these ascended
In flattening the prolonged candle flames,
Flung their smoke into the laquearia,
Stirring the pattern on the coffered ceiling.
Huge sea-wood fed with copper
95  Burned green and orange, framed by the colored stone,
In which sad light a carved dolphin swam.
Above the antique mantel was displayed
As though a window gave upon the sylvan scene
The change of Philomel, by the barbarous king
100  So rudely forced; yet there the nightingale
Filled all the desert with inviolable voice
And still she cried, and still the world pursues,
"Jug Jug" to dirty ears.
And other withered stumps of time
105  Were told upon the walls; staring forms
Leaned out, leaning, hushing the room enclosed.
Footsteps shuffled on the stair.
Under the firelight, under the brush, her hair
Spread out in fiery points
110  Glowed into words, then would be savagely still.

"My nerves are bad tonight. Yes, bad. Stay with me.
"Speak to me. Why do you never speak. Speak.
"What are you thinking of? What thinking? What?

 荒原

"I never know what you are thinking. Think."

115  I think we are in rats' alley
     Where the dead men lost their bones.

     "What is that noise?"
            The wind under the door.
     "What is that noise now? What is the wind doing?"
120                    Nothing again nothing.

                              "Do
     "You know nothing? Do you see nothing? Do you remember
     "Nothing?"

            I remember
125  Those are pearls that were his eyes.
     "Are you alive, or not? Is there nothing in your head?"
            But
     O O O O that Shakespeherian Rag---
     It's so elegant
130  So intelligent
        "What shall I do now? What shall I do?
     "I shall rush out as I am, and walk the street
     "With my hair down, so. What shall we do tomorrow?
     "What shall we ever do?"
135                    The hot water at ten.
     And if it rains, a closed car at four.
     And we shall play a game of chess,

Pressing lidless eyes and waiting for a knock upon the door.

When Lil's husband got demobbed, I said--
140    I didn't mince my words, I said to her myself,
HURRY UP PLEASE IT'S TIME
Now Albert's coming back, make yourself a bit smart.
He'll want to know what you done with that money he gave you
To get yourself some teeth. He did, I was there.
145    You have them all out, Lil, and get a nice set,
He said, I swear, I can't bear to look at you.
And no more can't I, I said, and think of poor Albert,
He's been in the army four years, he wants a good time,
And if you don't give it him, there's others will, I said.
150    Oh is there, she said. Something o' that, I said.
Then I'll know who to thank, she said, and give me a straight look.
HURRY UP PLEASE ITS TIME
If you don't like it you can get on with it, I said.
Others can pick and choose if you can't.
155    But if Albert makes off, it won't be for lack of telling.
You ought to be ashamed, I said, to look so antique.
(And her only thirty-one.)
I can't help it, she said, pulling a long face,
It's them pills I took, to bring it off, she said.
160    (She's had five already, and nearly died of young George.)
The chemist said it would be all right, but I've never been the same.
You are a proper fool, I said.

 荒原

  Well, if Albert won't leave you alone, there it is, I said,
  What you get married for if you don't want children?
165 HURRY UP PLEASE ITS TIME
  Well, that Sunday Albert was home, they had a hot gammon,
  And they asked me in to dinner, to get the beauty of it hot--
  HURRY UP PLEASE ITS TIME
  HURRY UP PLEASE ITS TIME
170 Goonight Bill. Goonight Lou. Goonight May. Goonight.
  Ta ta. Goonight. Goonight.
  Good night, ladies, good night, sweet ladies, good night, good night.

## III. The Fire Sermon

  The river's tent is broken: the last fingers of leaf
  Clutch and sink into the wet bank. The wind
175 Crosses the brown land, unheard. The nymphs are departed.
  Sweet Thames, run softly, till I end my song.
  The river bears no empty bottles, sandwich papers,
  Silk handkerchiefs, cardboard boxes, cigarette ends
  Or other testimony of summer nights. The nymphs are departed.
180 And their friends, the loitering heirs of City directors;
  Departed, have left no addresses.
  By the waters of Leman I Sat down and wept...
  Sweet Thames, run softly till I end my song,
  Sweet Thames, run softly, for I speak not loud or long.
185 But at my back in a cold blast I hear

 *The Waste Land*

The rattle of the bones, and chuckle spread from ear to ear.

      A rat crept softly through the vegetation
      Dragging its slimy belly on the bank
      While I was fishing in the dull canal
190  On a winter evening round behind the gashouse
      Musing upon the king my brother's wreck
      And on the king my father's death before him.
      White bodies naked on the low damp ground
      And bones cast in a little low dry garret,
195  Rattled by the rat's foot only, year to year.
      But at my back from time to time I hear
      The sound of horns and motors, which shall bring
      Sweeney to Mrs. Porter in the spring.
      O the moon shone bright on Mrs. Porter
200  And on her daughter
      They wash their feet in soda water
      *Et O ces voix d'enfants, chantant dans la coupole!*

      Twit twit twit
      Jug jug jug jug jug jug
205  So rudely forc'd.
      Terue

      Unreal City
      Under the brown fog of a winter noon
      Mr. Eugenides, the Smyrna merchant
210  Unshaven, with a pocket full of currants

 荒原

C.i.f. London: documents at sight,
Asked me in demotic French
To luncheon at the Cannon Street Hotel
Followed by a weekend at the Metropole.

215 At the violet hour, when the eyes and back
Turn upward from the desk, when the human engine waits
Like a taxi throbbing waiting,
I Tiresias, though blind, throbbing between two lives,
Old man with wrinkled female breasts, can see
220 At the violet hour, the evening hour that strives
Homeward, and brings the sailor home from sea,
The typist home at teatime, clears her breakfast, lights
Her stove, and lays out food in tins.
Out of the window perilously spread
225 Her drying combinations touched by the sun's last rays,
On the divan are piled (at night by her bed)
Stockings, slippers, camisoles, and stays.
I Tiresias, old man with wrinkled dugs
Perceived the scene, and foretold the rest--
230 I too awaited the expected guest.
He, the young man carbuncular, arrives,
A small house agent's clerk, with one bold stare,
One of the low on whom assurance sits
As a silk hat on a Bradford millionaire.
235 The time is now propitious, as he guesses,
The meal is ended, she is bored and tired,
Endeavors to engage her in caresses

Which still are unreproved, if undesired.
Flushed and decided, he assaults at once;
240 Exploring hands encounter no defense;
His vanity requires no response,
And makes a welcome of indifference.
(And I Tiresias have foresuffered all
Enacted on this same divan or bed;
245 I who have sat by Thebes below the wall
And walked among the lowest of the dead.)
Bestows one final patronizing kiss,
And gropes his way, finding the stairs unlit…

She turns and looks a moment in the glass,
250 Hardly aware of her departed lover;
Her brain allows one half-formed thought to pass:
"Well now that's done: and I'm glad it's over."
When lovely woman stoops to folly and
Paces about her room again, alone,
255 She smoothes her hair with automatic hand,
And puts a record on the gramophone.

"This music crept by me upon the waters"
And along the Strand, up Queen Victoria Street.
O City city, I can sometimes hear
260 Beside a public bar in Lower Thames Street,
The pleasant whining of a mandolin
And a clatter and a chatter from within
Where fishmen lounge at noon: where the walls

 荒原

      Of Magnus Martyr I hold
265    Inexplicable splendor of Ionian white and gold.

      The river sweats
      Oil and tar
      The barges drift
      With the turning tide
270    Red sails
      Wide
      To leeward, swing on the heavy spar.
      The barges wash
      Drifting logs
275    Down Greenwich reach
      Past the Isle of Dogs.
                     Weialala leia
                       Wallala leialala

      Elizabeth and Leicester
280    Beating oars
      The stern was formed
      A gilded shell
      Red and gold
      The brisk swell
285    Rippled both shores
      Southwest wind
      Carried down stream
      The peal of bells
      White towers
290                    Weialala leia

      Wallala leialala

"Trams and dusty trees.
Highbury bore me. Richmond and Kew
Undid me. By Richmond I raised my knees
Supine on the floor of a narrow canoe."

"My feet are at Moorgate, and my heart
Under my feet. After the event
He wept. He promised a new start.'
I made no comment. What should I resent?"

"On Margate Sands.
I can connect
Nothing with Nothing.
The broken fingernails of dirty hands.
My people humble people who expect
Nothing."
     la la

To Carthage then I came

Burning burning burning burning
O Lord Thou pluckest me out
O Lord Thou pluckest

burning

 荒原

## IV. Death by Water

Phlebas the Phoenician, a fortnight dead,
Forgot the cry of gulls, and the deep sea swell
And the profit and loss.
315    A current under sea
Picked his bones in whispers. As he rose and fell
He passed the stages of his age and youth
Entering the whirlpool.
        Gentle or Jew
320  O you who turn the wheel and look to windward,
Consider Phlebas, who was once handsome and tall as you.


## V. What the Thunder Said

After the torchlight red on sweaty faces
After the frosty silence in the gardens
After the agony in stony places
325  The shouting and the crying
Prison and palace and reverberation
Of thunder of spring over distant mountains
He who was living is now dead
We who were living are now dying
330  With a little patience

Here is no water but only rock
Rock and no water and the sandy road
The road winding above among the mountains

Which are mountains of rock without water
335 If there were water we should stop and drink
Amongst the rock one cannot stop or think
Sweat is dry and feet are in the sand
If there were only water amongst the rock
Dead mountain mouth of carious teeth that cannot spit
340 Here one can neither stand nor lie nor sit
There is not even silence in the mountains
But dry sterile thunder without rain
There is not even solitude in the mountains
But red sullen faces sneer and snarl
345 From doors of mudcracked houses

                          If there were water
   And no rock
   If there were rock
   And also water
   And water
350    A spring
   A pool among the rock
   If there were the sound of water only
   Not the cicada
   And dry grass singing
355    But sound of water over a rock
   Where the hermit thrush sings in the pine trees
   Drip drop drip drop drop drop drop
   But there is no water

 荒原

Who is the third who walks always beside you?
360  When I count, there are only you and I together
But when I look ahead up the white road
There is always another one walking beside you
Gliding wrapped in a brown mantle, hooded
I do not know whether a man of a woman
365  ---But who is that on the other side of you?

What is that sound high in the air
Murmur of maternal lamentation
Who are those hooded hordes swarming
Over endless plains, stumbling in cracked earth
370  Ringed by the flat horizon only
What is the city over the mountains
Cracks and reforms and bursts in the violet air
Falling towers
Jerusalem Athens Alexandria
375  Vienna London
Unreal

A woman drew her long black hair out tight
And fiddled whisper music on those strings
And bats with baby faces in the violet light
380  Whistled, and beat their wings
And crawled head downward down a blackened wall
And upside down in air were towers
Tolling reminiscent bells, that kept the hours
And voices singing out of empty cisterns and exhausted wells.

| | |
|---|---|
| 385 | In this decayed hole among the mountains |
| | In the faint moonlight, the grass is singing |
| | Over the tumbled graves, about the chapel |
| | There is the empty chapel, only the wind's home. |
| | It has no windows, and the door swings, |
| 390 | Dry bones can harm no one. |
| | Only a cock stood on the rooftree |
| | Co co rico co co rico |
| | In a flash of lightning. Then a damp gust |
| | Bringing rain |
| | |
| 395 | Ganga was sunken, and the limp leaves |
| | Waited for rain, while the black clouds |
| | Gathered far distant, over Himavant. |
| | The jungle crouched, humped in silence. |
| | Then spoke the thunder |
| 400 | Da |
| | Datta: what have we given? |
| | My friend, blood shaking my heart |
| | The awful daring of a moment's surrender |
| | Which an age of prudence can never retract |
| 405 | By this, and this only, we have existed |
| | Which is not to be found in our obituaries |
| | Or in memories draped by the beneficent spider |
| | Or under seals broken by the lean solicitor |
| | In our empty rooms |
| 410 | Da |

 荒原

        Dayadhvam: I have heard the key
        Turn in the door once and turn once only
        We think of the key, each in his prison
        Thinking of the key, each confirms a prison
415    Only at nightfall, ethereal rumors
        Revive for a moment a broken Coriolanus
        Da
        Damyata: The boat responded
        Gaily, to the hand expert with sail and oar
420    The sea was calm, your heart would have responded
        Gaily, when invited, beating obedient
        To controlling hands

                I sat upon the shore
        Fishing, with the arid plain behind me
425    Shall I at least set my lands in order?
        London Bridge is falling down falling down falling down
        *Poi s'ascose nel foco che gli affina*
        *Quando fiam uti chelidon*---O swallow swallow
        *Le Prince d'Aquitainte a la tour abolie*
430    These fragments I have shored against my ruins
        Why then Ile fit you. Hieronymo's mad againe.
        Datta. Dayadhvam. Damyata.

            Shantih    shantih    shantih

# NOTES

Not only the title, but the plan and a good deal of the incidental symbolism of the poem were suggested by Miss Jessie L. Weston's book on the Grail legend: *From Ritual to Romance* (Cambridge). Indeed, so deeply am I indebted, Miss Weston's book will elucidate the difficulties of the poem much better than my notes can do; and I recommend it (apart from the great interest of the book itself) to any who think such elucidation of the poem worth the trouble. To another work of anthropology I am indebted in general, one which has influenced our generation profoundly; I mean *The Golden Bough*; I have used especially the two volumes *Adonis, Attis, Osiris*. Anyone who is acquainted with these works will immediately recognize in the poem certain references to vegetation ceremonies.

I. Burial of the Dead

20. Cf. Ezekiel II, i.

23. Cf. Ecclesiastes XII, v.

31. V. Tristan und Isolde, I, verses 5-8.

42. [V. Tristan und Isolde,] III, verse 24.

46. I am not familiar with the exact constitution of the Tarot pack of cards, from which I have obviously departed to suit my own convenience. The Hanged Man, a member of the traditional pack, fits my purpose in two ways: because he is associated in my mind with the Hanged God of Frazer, and because I associate him with the hooded

 荒原

figure in the passage of the disciples to Emmaus in Part V. The Phoenician Sailor and the Merchant appear later; also the "crowds of people," and Death by Water is executed in Part IV. The Man with Three Staves (an authentic member of the Tarot pack) I associate, quite arbitrarily, with the Fisher King himself.

60. Cf. Baudelaire

> "Fourmillante cité, cité pleine de rêves,
> "Où le spectre en plein jour raccroche le passant."

63. Cf. Inferno III, 55-57:

> "si lunga tratta
> di gente, ch'io non avrei mai creduto
> che morte tanta n'avesse disfatta."

64. Cf. Inferno IV, 25-27:

> "Quivi, secondo che per ascoltare,
> non avea pianto ma' che de sospiri,
> che l'aura eterna facevan tremare."

68. A phenomenon which I have often noticed.

74. Cf. the Dirge in Webster's *White Devil*.

76. V. Baudelaire, Preface to *Fleurs du Mal*.

77. Cf. *Antony and Cleopatra*, II, ii, l. 190.

II. A Game of Chess

92. Laquearia. V. *Aeneid*, I, 726:

> dependent lychni laquearibus incensi
> aureis, et noctem flammis funalia vincunt

98. Sylvan scene. V. Milton, *Paradise Lost*, IV, 140.

99. V. Ovid, *Metamorphoses*, VI, Philomela.

100. Cf. Part III, l. 204.

115. Cf. Part III, l. 195.

118. Cf. Webster: "Is the wind in that door still?"

126. Cf. Part I, 37, 48.

138. Cf. The game of chess in Middleton's *Women Beware Women*.

## III. The Fire Sermon

176. V. Spenser, *Prothalamion*.

192. Cf. *The Tempest*, I, ii.

196. Cf. Marvell, *To His Coy Mistress*.

197. Cf. Day, *Parliament of Bees*:

> "When of the sudden, listening, you shall hear,
> "A noise of horns and hunting, which shall bring
> "Actaeon to Diana in the spring,
> "Where all shall see her naked skin…"

 荒原

199. I do not know the origin of the ballad from which these lines are taken: it was reported to me from Sydney, Australia.

202. V. Verlaine, *Parsifal*.

210. The currants were quoted at a price "carriage and insurance free to London"; and the Bill of Lading etc. were to be handed to the buyer upon payment of the sight draft.

218. Tiresias, although a mere spectator and not indeed a "character," is yet the most important personage in the poem, uniting all the rest. Just as the one-eyed merchant, seller of currants, melts into the Phoenician Sailor, and the latter is not wholly distinct from Ferdinand Prince of Naples, so all the women are one woman, and the two sexes meet in Tiresias. What Tiresias *sees*, in fact, is the substance of the poem. The whole passage from Ovid is of great anthropological interest:

> '…Cum Iunone iocos et maior vestra profecto est
> Quam, quae contingit maribus,' dixisse, 'voluptas.'
> Illa negat; placuit quae sit sententia docti
> Quaerere Tiresiae: venus huic erat ultraque nota.
> Nam duo magnorum viridi coeuntia silva
> Corpora serpentum baculi violaverat ictu
> Deque viro factus, mirabile, femina septem
> Egerat autumnos; octavo rursus eosdem
> Vidit et 'est vestrae si tanta potentia plagae,'
> Dixit 'ut auctoris sortem in contraria mutet,
> Nunc quoque vos feriam!' percussis anguibus isdem
> Forma prior rediit genetivaque venit imago.
> Arbiter hic igitur sumptus de lite iocosa
> Dicta Iovis firmat; gravius Saturnia iusto
> Nec pro materia fertur doluisse suique

Iudicis aeterna damnavit lumina nocte,
At pater omnipotens (neque enim licet inrita cuiquam
Facta dei fecisse deo) pro lumine adempto
Scire futura dedit poenamque levavit honore.

221. This may not appear as exact as Sappho's lines, but I had in mind "longshore" or "dory" fisherman, who returns at nightfall.

253. V. Goldsmith, the song in *The Vicar of Wakefield*.

257. V. *The Tempest*, as above.

264. The interior of St. Magnus Martyr is to my mind one of the finest among Wren's interiors. See *The Proposed Demolition of Nineteen City Churches*: (P. S. King & Sons, Ltd.)

266. The Song of the (three) Thames-daughters begins here. From line 292 to 306 inclusive they speak in turn. V. *Götterdämmerung*, III, i: the Rhine-daughters.

279. V. Froude, *Elizabeth*, Vol. I, ch. iv, letter of De Quadra to Philip of Spain:

> "In the afternoon we were in a barge, watching the games on the river. (The queen) was alone with Lord Robert and myself on the poop, when they began to talk nonsense, and went so far that Lord Robert at last said, as I was on the spot there was no reason why they should not be married if the queen pleased."

293. Cf. *Purgatorio*, V, 133:

> "Ricorditi di me, che son la Pia;
> "Siena mi fe', disfecemi Maremma."

 荒原

307. V. St. Augustine's *Confessions*: "to Carthage then I came, where a cauldron of unholy loves sang all about mine ears."

308. The complete text of the Buddha's Fire Sermon (which corresponds in importance to the Sermon on the Mount) from which these words are taken, will be found translated in the late Henry Clarke Warren's *Buddhism in Translation* (Harvard Oriental Series). Mr. Warren was one of the great pioneers of Buddhist studies in the Occident.

309. From St. Augustine's *Confessions* again. The collocation of these two representatives of eastern and western ascetism, as the culmination of this part of the poem, is not an accident.

V. What the Thunder Said

In the first part of Part V three themes are employed: the journey to Emmaus, the approach to the Chapel Perilous (see Miss Weston's book) and the present decay of eastern Europe.

357. This is *Turdus aonalaschkae pallasii*, the hermit-thrush which I have heard in Quebec County. Chapman says (*Handbook of Birds of Eastern North America*) "it is most at home in secluded woodland and thickety retreats... Its notes are not remarkable for variety or volume, but in purity and sweetness of tone and exquisite modulation they are unequalled." Its "water-dripping song" is justly celebrated.

360. The following lines were stimulated by the account of one of the Antarctic expeditions (I forget which, but I think one of Shackleton's): it was related that the party of explorers, at the extremity of their strength, had the constant delusion that there was *one more member* than could actually be counted.

366-376. Cf. Hermann Hesse, *Blick ins chaos*:

"Schon ist halb Europa, schon ist zumindest der halbe Osten Europas auf dem Wege zum Chaos, fährt betrunken im heiligem Wahn am Abgrund entlang und singt dazu, singt betrunken und hymnisch wie Dmitri Karamasoff sang. Ueber diese Lieder lacht der Bürger beleidigt, der Heilige und Seher hört sie mit Tränen."

401. "Datta, dayadhvam, damyata" (Give, sympathise, control). The fable of the meaning of the Thunder is found in the *Brihadaranyaka—Upanishad*, 5, 1. A translation is found in Deussen's Sechsig *Upanishads des Veda*, p. 489.

407. Cf. Webster, *The White Devil*, V, vi:

"...they'll remarry
Ere the worm pierce your winding-sheet, ere the spider
Make a thin curtain for your epitaphs."

411. Cf. *Inferno*, XXXIII, 46:

"ed io sentii chiavar l'uscio di sotto
all'orribile torre."

Also F. H. Bradley, *Appearance and Reality*, p. 346:

 荒原

"My external sensations are no less private to myself than are my thoughts or my feelings. In either case my experience falls within my own circle, a circle closed on the outside; and, with all its elements alike, every sphere is opaque to the others which surround it... In brief, regarded as an existence which appears in a soul, the whole world for each is peculiar and private to that soul."

424. V. Weston: *From Ritual to Romance*; chapter on the Fisher King.

427. V. *Purgatorio*, XXVI, 148.

> "'Ara vos prec, per aquella valor
> 'que vos guida al som de l'escalina,
> 'sovegna vos a temps de ma dolor.'
> Poi s'ascose nel foco che gli affina."

428. V. *Pervigilium Veneris*. Cf. Philomela in Parts II and III.

429. V. Gerard de Nerval, Sonnet *El Desdichado*.

431. V. Kyd's *Spanish Tragedy*.

433. Shantih. Repeated as here, a formal ending to an Upanishad. "The Peace which passeth understanding" is a feeble translation of the content of the word.

# 《荒原》翻译要点

本书《前言》中提到现存《荒原》译本，虽然都是各位大家呕心沥血的力作，但仍有许多值得进一步深入理解和体味的余地，包括内容和形式、理解和转达等多个层面。这些都表现在具体的译文中。笔者在翻译过程中注意到并努力改善这些具体问题，探究的同时也做了笔记。没有这些探究和发现，这个译本就不能成篇。本着知无不言的讨论精神，特此把翻译手记奉上，就诗歌文本中这些具体的要点谈一谈笔者的体察和拙译的考量。

\* \* \* \*

题词：原文为拉丁文夹希腊文："NAM sibyllam quidem Cuimis ego ipse oculis meis vidi in ampulla pendere, et cum illi pueri dicerent: Σιβνλλατιθελειζ; repondebat illa: αποθαν ειν θελω." 诗人把其中"Σιβνλλατιθελειζ"译作"What do you want?"，而"What"既可以指"什么"，也可以指"怎样"。在这里偏重后者，整句意为"你有什么愿望或想法"，故译作"你想要咋样"。（另有英译为"What do you wish"，"I wish to die"，则更为明确。）

献词："艺高一筹"：意大利原文"il miglior fabbro"

来自但丁《神曲》，多个英文版本都用了比较级（"better smith"及"fairer ornament"），在中文里也应得到相应的体现；译文脱离字面结构，采用"归化"译法，而弃用含义欠信、文字欠顺的逐字翻译。

一、葬亡

标题"葬亡"：原文"The Burial of the Dead"与英国国教的葬礼祷告词的标题 *The Burial of the Dead* 文字相同。Burial 一词来自动词 bury，本意为"埋葬"，延申可指"埋葬的仪式"（funeral）；查整诗蕴涵，并无仪式痕迹，取本意；而"the dead"除了指人，亦应暗含诗中描述的死的地、死的树、死的山、死的钟声等，更暗指精神的死亡；二者合译"葬亡"。

第一段：原诗使用的时态，从一般现在时起始，继而转为一般过去时，再转到过去的某些具体时空——这里时态的转换是有含义的；内容从泛谈"April"，到泛说过去和身份不明的"us"，再到"we"的具体动态及具体地点；从静到动，从无人称到"我们"到叙述者"我"。行文一步步展开，一步步具象化，在时间上却是反向进行。这有点像黑白影片化入彩色倒叙。诗人如此设计必有用意：四月春天到了，现实在眼前，它是死亡般严酷；而此前的冬天，尚可于覆雪之下暂且忘掉现实的寒冷，感觉还有一点生机；再往前，那个夏天突然"携雨而至"，应是暗喻一战爆发，让醉生梦死的皇族（后来亮明"我们"的身份为奥匈帝国皇族）吃了一惊。一战之后，满目疮痍，欧洲败落成为"荒原"，今不如昔，曾经身为贵族的叙述者"我"感受深切。时间的倒置，以及今天的死沉沉和过去的活生生（紧接着，行文的时序进一步倒退到叙述者以及皇储表兄家的生活）二者之间的反差，都紧扣整首诗的主题。译文力图建立三个时间段的立体感，用"冬天**保了**我们温暖……夏天**给了**我们一惊"把原文中时态转换的内涵表达出来，让它像在原文中一样服务主题。

12 行："我可不是俄罗斯人，我来自立陶宛，正宗日耳曼人"：原文为德文"Bin gar keine Russin, stamm' aus Litauen, echt deutsch"，英文作"I am not Russian at all; I come from Lithuania, a true German"。从人物原型看，如果说话者就是艾略特曾与之会面的玛丽·路易斯·拉里施伯爵夫人，如评家所言，则她出生在巴伐利亚（当时不属于德国），是奥地利皇室近亲；从人物自述看，她表兄大公是奥匈帝国王储，她"来自立陶宛"（远离德国）；从内容看，她自称"deutsch"强调的不会是国籍，而是种族和血统认同，带有种族自傲（是为引发一战的民族主义情绪）。三者都与德国无关，故将"deutsch"译作"德国人"是不正确的。

19-20 行："有什么根会紧抓这烂石堆，有什么枝会/从这烂石堆中长出来？"：原文是"What are the roots that clutch, what branches grow/Out of this stony rubbish?"其中，"clutch"的逻辑宾语也是"this stony rubbish"。参考其最可能的出典《圣经·旧约·约伯记》第 8 章第 17 节："他的根盘绕石堆，钻入石缝。"

31-34 行：

"清风习习地吹呀

荒原

吹到我家乡
我那爱尔兰姑娘呀
你留连在何方？"

这是瓦格纳歌剧《特里斯坦与伊索尔德》中水手在海上思念女友时唱的歌。译文意图用歌谣式的朴实语言，移植歌词原有的节律和韵式，传达它如泣如诉的悲凉之感。

45行："通神"：原文"wise"一词旧有"通巫术、通神、有魔力"之义，被诗人妙用于此，一语双关，讥锋暗露；简单译作"智慧"则有失明察，且有违语境。可参考第43行译者注。

46行："手握一副诡妙的纸牌"原文为"With a wicked pack of cards"。这里"with"动词感强，而"wicked"一词含有邪恶和妙算之意；音韵方面，与前一行"wisest woman"都用了头韵，译文没有、也难以刻意追求。

48行："那些明珠原是他的眼睛"：源出莎士比亚《暴风雨》第一幕第二场中爱丽儿的丧歌"Those are pearls that were his eyes"。其中前后两个动词时态对比明显，译文用"原是"表现时间和人事的纵向反差：时过人亡。诗中多处运用这种抚今追昔之法：全诗第一段的时间倒叙，以及第四章中"腓尼基人弗莱巴，死了已经两星期……他也曾高大英俊"，等，都是实例。是不是让人想到"陋室空堂，当年笏满床；衰草枯杨，曾为歌舞场"？中英名著两部，技法如出一辙。

49行："贝拉东纳（Belladonna）"一词源于意大利语bella donna，意为"漂亮女人"，是一种植物（颠茄），可制眼用化妆品，也是一种毒药，其中"donna"

暗含圣母，或许含意双关；"岩间女士（the Lady of the Rocks）"暗指达芬奇作品《岩间圣母》（*Virgin of the Rocks*）和《蒙娜丽莎》（*Mona Lisa*），在下一行又转成"lady of situations"；综合起来，应该代表了诗中各种情景下的女性人物（参考诗人原注第218行）。其变化并非主动，也没有明显的贬义。未作"随机应变"，而译作"随情就景的女士"。

55行：塔罗牌中的倒悬者（一译"倒吊人"）原文为"The Hanged Man"，是一只脚倒挂在丁字树上的自我牺牲者，以便重生之日为大地带来丰产。他不是"被绞死"或"被吊死"的；"当心溺亡水中"：原文"Fear death by water"是祈使句，警告有落水溺死之险。

60-66行：这里有一段较长的插入成分，应理解为置于破折号之间，作："诡异的城啊，/在冬日拂晓的褐色雾中，/一群人流过伦敦桥，——那么多人，/没想到死神竟报销了那么多人。/悲叹，短促的悲叹，偶而嘘出，/每个人都把眼睛盯在脚前面。/——流上街坡又流下威廉王大街"。

60行："诡异的城啊"：艾略特在原注中让读者参看波德莱尔的诗《七个老头》："Fourmillante cité, cité pleine de rêves,/Où le spectre en plein jour raccroche le passant（人群涌动的城，充满迷梦的城，/那里幽灵在光天化日下搭讪过路的人）"。这个描述很可能也与汤普森诗 *The City of Dreadful Night* 相关。褐色晨雾弥漫，一群行尸走肉在街上流动，没有灵魂，死沉的钟声，幽灵在搭讪路人，岂不诡异乎？而且在下文中，说话者遇见千年以前死亡的战友，进一步暗指这座城如同但丁笔

 荒原

下可以遇见亡魂的地狱，这岂是一个"不真实"或者"虚幻"可以了得？原文"unreal"从字面上看虽为 real 的反义词，然而含义却更为丰富。查 Oxford Advanced Learner's Dictionary 释义 unreal 一词，其中第一意为："so strange that it is more like a dream than reality"，本义就是"怪异"，并强调了怪异的程度。故它字面之下的深层信息，需要身入语境去感受。

66 行："流上街坡"：原文"Flowed up the hill"。这一小段描绘的是伦敦街道实景，而从伦敦桥到威廉王大街，只是城市街道，其间并没有"山"或"山岗"，阅读和翻译时当有所查。

二、棋局

标题中原文"Chess"译作"棋"，而未用以中华文化中的围棋为本意的"弈"。

77-82 行："镜子/撑在镂着果实藤蔓的框柱中，/藤蔓中有个金色丘比特向外探望/（另一个把眼睛藏在翅膀里）/将七枝烛台的火苗翻倍"当读作"镜子——/撑在镂着果实藤蔓的框柱中，/藤蔓中有个金色丘比特向外探望/（另一个把眼睛藏在翅膀里）——/将七枝烛台的火苗翻倍"。如前所述，艾略特常用较长的插入成分，诗中多有这种结构。

关于这一段中的另一特点，即，词语修饰关系的多重可能性及诗中某词词性的朦胧性，威廉·燕卜荪（William Empson）在其《朦胧的七种类型》（Seven Types of Ambiguity）中曾以从 77 到 93 行这一段作为例子，加以说明。类似的例子诗中还有很多。不过笔者认

为，燕卜荪的说明主要表现在语法修饰关系上，其中有些例子尽管有着这些朦胧和多重修饰的可能，从逻辑关系上还是可以分析出主次的。中文翻译尤其难以全面照顾，拙译即根据逻辑分析做了选择。当然，多样并行和主次有序这两种理解并不一定就相互矛盾：多义和朦胧都是诗歌的特权。

89-90 行："窗口空气/清新袭来"译自"air that freshened from the window"，盖因关键词"freshen"含有风力增强、空气变鲜、提振精神等意。诗中情景实为新鲜空气含氧较丰，吹进来使火苗燃烧更旺。

94 行："浸了铜盐的巨块海漂木/燃出绿色和橙色"：这里描述的是第 97 行中提到的"古旧的壁炉"中的情景：海漂木经海水浸泡后留在上面的铜盐燃烧时呈绿色。故而前人所译"木料撒上铜粉"或"铜制的海洋森林"，"木器镶满了黄铜"，"海水浸过的柴，撒着铜粉"，"沉香木用铜皿供奉着"等，则离开了语境，发挥了过多的想象力和创造力，皆属误解误译。

95 行："色彩映在石框上"：壁炉石边框住了火，如同镜框框着图画。

94-96 行：继续描述"她"那堂皇而古旧的大厅中的情景：巨大的壁炉由光亮的大理石砌成，炉中浸着铜盐的海漂木燃烧出绿色和橘色的火苗，映照在石框的表面；有一大块被海浪冲刷而酷似海豚的海漂木在燃烧，看着令人悲伤。把握了整个段落所描绘的场景及其意图，具体的难懂之处就会迎刃而解。

102 行："她恒久地呼喊，而世界至今在驱赶/"啾啾"，对着那肮脏的耳朵"应读作"她恒久地呼喊——

而世界至今在驱赶——"啾啾",对着那肮脏的耳朵。"。其原文"And still she cried, and still the world pursues"中,两个"still"含义略有不同,且动词时态反差强烈。前者一词双关,译文未敢舍弃任何一个。

129-130 行:"多么雅致/多么机智"对应原文 It's so elegant/So intelligent 的节奏、谐音加叠韵。

138 行:"撑着眼皮"原文"Pressing lidless eyes"中"press"是强撑的意思,"lidless"直解是没有眼皮,实则是看不到能合上或者偶尔眨眼的眼皮。直译容易误解。

153 行:"就算你不乐意,也将就些吧,我说。/别人能挑三拣四,你可没得挑"来自原文"If you don't like it you can get on with it, I said./Others can pick and choose if you can't"。这里 it 应该是指前面"好好快活一下,你要是不给他,有人会给的"中的两个意思,或其中任何一个;大意是说,对这种事,就算你不受用,也得过且过吧;别人能挑选男人,你可没得挑,别弄到他跟人跑了。

### 三、火诫

186 行:"咧笑咯咯出声":原文"chuckle spread from ear to ear"中"from ear to ear"是熟语,指咧嘴大笑的样子;原文虽有"spread"一词,但在"背后的寒风中白骨咔咔作响"的意境中,很难有"从耳朵传到耳朵"的可能,而更像是出于节拍和押韵的考量。

229 行:"觉察到这一幕"译自"Perceived the scene"。提瑞舍斯是盲人,与其说"看到"不如说"觉察到"。

原文中这一行与下一行同押一韵，故以"下文"对"客人"。

230行："预期的客人"：原文中"expected"按字面可理解为"知道要来的"或"期待中的"，逻辑主语应为打字员，而非提瑞舍斯，这里多有误解错译；而体会语境，如果译作"期待"则有失之心切之虞。

231行："那个年轻轻的粉刺脸"：原文为"the young man carbuncular"，这种修饰手法带有挖苦的意味，译文设法与之对应。

235行："据他猜测"：原文"as he guesses"不应理解为"他猜对了"，这里只是叙述而没有兀突的判断。

242行："一厢情愿把冷漠当成乐意"。原文为"And makes a welcome of indifference"，使用的是短语"make something (out) of something"，例如成语"make a virtue of necessity"。因而"还欢迎这种漠然的神情"，和"却招来一种满不在乎的欢迎"等都是不应出现的误解误译。

259行："伦敦城"即 The City，指伦敦金融区，并不是任何城市，也不是简单的任何一个"城"，这一点已经得到广泛认识。

269行："随着退潮"：对原文"with the turning tide"的理解多有含混不清，将之译作"顺着来浪"，"随着潮流变换"，"随着浪起"，等。

273行："画舫浪拍/漂流的原木"：其原文"The barges wash/Drifting logs"中的 wash 含义双关：漂和冲。可理解为"the barges wash away down the river like, or along with, or making splashes against, drifting logs"。这样更可合情景，也更赋寓意。

279-80 行:"伊丽莎白和莱斯特/击水的船桨",其原文中"Elizabeth and Leicester/Beating oars"两行的文字是平行关系,不是主谓宾关系;伊丽莎白一世女王和莱斯特伯爵所乘的是大型豪阔的御用画舫,二人正在船尾甲板上调情,旁边还有一个当电灯泡的西班牙驻英大使。以其女王之尊,她会去亲手划桨摇橹吗?再说,这种要由二十人划桨的大船,此二尊又如何划得动?

292 行:"来往的电车灰土土的树":原文"Trams and dusty trees"。读时力图进入其场景,体会其情绪,感受到英文简单词语中所含的情感内涵;译文依据歌者身份采用底层人的朴实语言和节奏,而不敢仅停留在逐字对译上。

301-302 行:"我头脑空空,什么联想都没有。"原文为"I can connect/Nothing with nothing"。试想一下,尤其是联系到下文再体会一下,诗人表达的是什么呢?我把什么事物都联系不到一块,脑子一片空白,一脑袋糨子,失去了思维能力;头脑空空是诗中主题之一,如第 126 行"你脑壳里啥也没有吗?"如果把这一句硬译作"我能把乌有和乌有(或虚无和虚无)联系起来",而作为"直译"的标本,就好像把熟语"put two and two together"译作"把二和二放在一起",窃以为还是很难转达原意的。另,诗人如此行文或者还有押韵的考虑,后文将详加讨论。

四、溺亡

317 行:"他穿过一生每个阶段穿过青春":原文"He passed the stages of his age and youth"语法上可以

有两种理解,即寿命的各个阶段以及青春,或老年和青春两个阶段。我采用前者,不仅因为这样意义更恰当,更因为得到艾略特本人的佐证。这一段文字来自艾略特1918年所作法文诗《在餐馆》,如下:

Phlebas, le Phénicien, pendant quinze jours noyé,
Oubliait les cris des moutette et la houle de Cornouaille,
Et les profits et les pertes, et la cargaison d'étain:
Un courant de sous-mer l'emporta très loin,
Le repassant aux étapes de sa vie antérieure.
Figurez-vous donc, c'était un sort pénible;
Cependant, ce fut jadis un bel homme, de haute taille.

法文原作试译如下:

腓尼基人弗莱巴,溺亡已经十五天,
忘了鸥鸟的叫声,忘了康沃尔海的浪涌
也忘了盈利和亏损,和一货舱罐头:
一股洋流载他去远方,
把他带到前世的各个阶段。
试想吧,这么悲惨的命运;
然而,他也曾高大英俊。

五、雷之语

第331-358行:1923年8月,艾略特写信给福特·马多克斯·福特(Ford Madox Ford),提到《荒原》有大约30行佳句,看他能不能找出。10月,艾略特将这些佳句明确为这29行滴水之歌。笔者下笔翻译时尤为不敢怠慢，韵法、节奏、诗意、中文顺畅，多方考量。

345行："但愿能有水"：原文"If there were water"实为"If only there were water"之略，表示与实际情况不符的愿望，而不是条件句。可对照第335行条件句"要是能有水咱就停步把水喝（If there were water we should stop and drink）"，和第338行表示愿望的"多么渴望石头之间能有水（If there were only water amongst the rock）"，该行应为"If only there were water amongst the rock"的倒装。这一段文字，尤其是其中这两种句法的区别，是应该弄清楚的。

366-7行："那是什么声音凄厉在空中/可是慈母哀伤的喃喃声"：调研中读到的两处转述分别为"What is that high-pitched sound in the air, motherly wails？"，"What is the sound coming from the air in the distance which Sound like the cries of uprooted mothers？"都有问号，而诗中没有标点，似乎有意置于疑问和肯定之间。另，"high"一词主要是指高尖的女声，但同时也含一种来自高空的感觉，又一处一词双关。

385行："在这群山环抱的残破山沟"：原文中"hole"应指山谷，这个蹩脚的地方，而不是山洞。山洞里不会有月光、野草、坟茔和凶险教堂；而且在不同版本的故事中，圣杯骑士都是在森林里找到凶险教堂的。

399-400行："于是雷发话了/哒"。经核对徐梵澄、黄宝生两个译本，以及多个英文版本，《大森林奥义书》关于雷声意义的三种理解"哒"，顺序皆为：天神理解为"damyata"（自制），凡人理解为"datta"（施舍），阿修罗理解为"dayadhvam"（仁慈）；而赵萝蕤和汤永宽两个版本的注释与上不同，皆为神理解为"datta"、阿修罗理解为"Dāmyata"、人理解为"dayadhvam"，未知何故。

403-404 行：初稿译作："一时放任的莽撞之举/一世的谨慎都无法挽回"，后改为："这顷刻间舍弃的非凡勇气/一世审慎也无法撤回的勇气"，反映了笔者在不同时段参考多家解读并对比思考的过程。语法上，第二行其实是第一行的补充修饰，并非谓语，同时予以改正。

433 末行："玄静"原文 Shantih 意为和平，平安，寂静等。艾略特引《圣经·新约》文字 "The Peace which passeth understanding" 为之作注，可见诗人赋予它玄妙的精神内涵，故有拙译。后查考"玄静"其词，谓"清静无为的思想境界"，"犹安定，平静"，再次确认。又例：《晋书·裴秀传》中有"玄静守真，性入道奥"；清刘献廷《广阳杂记》卷三中有"道德通玄静，真常守太清"。

\* \* \* \*

回头再说说音韵的处理。作为现代诗，这首长诗总体上用的是没有韵律的自由体；但诗作的很多段落却节奏齐整，合辙押韵。比如全诗开篇的头几行，就采用了扬抑格和弱音节尾韵：

April / is the / cruellest / month, breeding
Lilacs / out of / the dead / land, mixing

 荒原

Memo / ry and / desire, stirring
Dull roots / with spring / rain.

译文有意识地在不影响语义和顺畅的前提下,最大程度地移植这种节奏感和弱尾韵:

四月 之月 最是 残酷,把
丁香 在那 死地上 滋育,把
记忆 和欲望 搅作 一团,把
麻木 的根 用春雨 拨弄。

而更常见的是,在一些段落,诗人用韵律取得加强语气、变换口吻、往往语含讥讽的效果。译文也有意遵循这种安排,在大多数情况下,尽量采用同样格式,也就是在节奏和韵式上与原文相仿。如下面这段就大篇幅地用韵:

The time is now propitious, as he guesses,
The meal is ended, she is bored and tired,
Endeavors to engage her in caresses
Which still are unreproved, if undesired.
Flushed and decided, he assaults at once;
Exploring hands encounter no defense;
His vanity requires no response,
And makes a welcome of indifference.
(And I Tiresias have foresuffered all
Enacted on this same divan or bed;
I who have sat by Thebes below the wall
And walked among the lowest of the dead.)

翻译要点

Bestows one final patronizing kiss,
And gropes his way, finding the stairs unlit…

此刻时机很有利,据他猜测,
饭已吃完但见她,厌烦困乏,
探手探脚拉过来搂抱亲热,
虽未见她来相迎也没遭骂。
脸一红来心一横立刻进攻;
上下其手去摸索没遇抗拒;
他那虚荣不需要任何回应,
一厢情愿把冷漠当成乐意。
(而我提瑞舍斯,早已领受过
这沙发这床榻演出的所有;
我曾在底比斯的城墙下坐,
也曾在最卑微的死人中走。)
临行把那最后一吻施舍上,
便摸着去路,只见楼梯没照亮……

这里大段引文的意图,不知读者是否已经察觉。其实,只要仔细读一遍,就可以发现,如上所引的从235到248的整个14行,遵循的是莎士比亚式十四行诗的格式,即五步抑扬格加 ABAB CDCD EFEF GG 韵式(原文最后两行属于半押韵)。这样古雅有致的形式装入诗人笔下现代人低劣无聊的作为,对照之下,戏谑意图令人莞尔。这样的韵律当然不会是无意所为,其功效也是显而易见的。拙译虽经努力,也难以达到格律完全整齐——或许也没有充分的必要追求完全整齐,但也采用了

 荒原

原作滑稽模仿的音韵形式,以期取得同样的讥锋暗露的效果。

另外一个例子,是三首泰晤士河女儿歌(从292行到306行)。原文每一首都各自押韵。三首合为一体正好又是一首完整的十四行诗的降格作品:韵式为ABAB CDCD EFG EFG,节奏上却是嘈嘈切切、断续杂连——以此烘托内容,实在是恰如其分。笔者译后才发现译文中三首歌竟压了统一的韵,于是顺势用它替代原作十四行诗韵式,而起到其串联效果,想来也无不可吧。

除此而外,整首诗中还含有另一个十四行诗段落,笔者也有意识地遵循原文格式加以处理,这里不再赘述,留给读者去明察体味。我只想指出这三首变体十四行诗的存在和诗人对诗歌格律的化用;这样的改造和化用也存在于其他韵律段落。

除了规整的韵律,在有些情况下,原诗用韵可谓自由组合。为了不损害语义,不影响译文顺畅,译文也选择了自由组合的用韵方式,而没有刻板地追求原诗的用韵结构。如下例:

> After the torchlight red on sweaty faces
> After the frosty silence in the gardens
> After the agony in stony places
> The shouting and the crying
> Prison and palace and reverberation
> Of thunder of spring over distant mountains
> He who was living is now dead
> We who were living are now dying
> With a little patience

火炬映红汗淋淋的脸庞过后
果园那寒霜般的寂静过后
乱石之间历经的磨难
监牢宫殿中的
哭叫呼喊还有远山
春雷的回响都过去之后
那位曾经活着的现在已经死去
我们曾经活着的现在正在死去
只在耐心等候

对于这一段，译文把原文的押韵结构作了些改变。由于中英文句法习惯的不同，前三行的"排比"句式后置，与尾韵结合；把原文一、三行及二、六、九行的总共五行两韵，改造为总共八行三韵，即一、二、六、九行压韵，中间夹有两处换韵。这样处理后，总体上应能与原文的音韵效果相当。

其实既然原诗处于从古典的韵律诗向自由体的现代诗转型过程中，原诗的音韵也明显脱离了严格的定式，而更加自由化；另外，诗中一些段落用韵还展现出一种相对的零散化（或许呼应了现代世界的零落？），因而译文同样处理，似乎也不无所循。原诗用韵和节奏也还有其他多种情形，以上仅举几例。用韵与否、如何用韵都只是手段，而达意传神才是目的。译文也应该充分关注到这些手段并尽量采用相同或相似的手段，以便达到达意传神的目的。

# J.阿尔弗雷德·普鲁弗洛克的情歌

假如我相信我的话是回答
一个终究会返回世上的人,
这团火焰就会静止不摇曳了;
但是,既然果真像我听到的那样,
从来没有人从这深渊中生还,
我就不怕名誉扫地来回答你。[a]


那咱就去吧,你和我,
夜幕已经在天空展扩
像个病人麻醉在手术台;

---

[a] 题词出自但丁《神曲·地狱篇》第27首,原文如下:
　　"S'io credesse che mia risposta fosse
　　A persona che mai tornasse al mondo,
　　Questa fiamma staria senza piu scosse.
　　Ma percioche giammai di questo fondo
　　Non torno vivo alcun, s'i'odo il vero,
　　Senza tema d'infamia ti rispondo"。
所引中文为田德望译本。艾略特引化身火焰的圭多这一段话,实为暗示普鲁弗洛克也像圭多一样,正身处地狱——现代社会的人间地狱而不能逃出,因而表露心迹也同样不怕丢人了。
\* 脚注均为译者所加。

The Love Song of J. Alfred Prufrock

  咱去吧，穿过些半遭遗弃的街巷，
5  那嘈杂可退歇的地方
  尽是勉强熬一宿的廉价客栈
  和到处蚝壳、满地锯末的餐馆：
  那些街巷一条接一条
  像居心叵测冗长乏味的呱噪
10  直把你引向一个令人窘迫的问题……
  哦，别问"是啥呀？"
  咱去探访一下吧。

  房间里女人们来往穿梭
  谈论着米开朗琪罗。

15  那黄雾用背磨蹭着玻璃窗，
  那黄烟用吻磨蹭着玻璃窗，
  把舌头舔进夜晚的角落，
  游弋在阴沟的水洼上，
  任烟囱里落下的煤烟落在背上，
20  它轻轻溜过露台，突然一跳，
  见那是十月温柔的一夜，
  便盘绕着房子，睡着了觉。

  也确实会有时间
  让那沿着街巷游弋的黄烟，
25  用背去磨蹭玻璃窗；

会有时间，会有时间
去备好一张脸去见你见的那些脸；
会有时间去谋杀去创建，ᵃ
有时间让循日劳作的双手ᵇ
30    去拈起问题放在你的餐盘；
有你的时间，有我的时间，
还有时间一百次地犹豫不定，
一百次地构想一百次地修正，
在取用吐司和茶水之前。

35    房间里女人们来往穿梭
谈论着米开朗琪罗。


也确实会有时间
去疑虑，"我敢不敢？""我敢不敢？"
有掉头走下楼梯的时间，
40    带着头顶那块脱发秃斑——
（她们会说："他的头发稀成这样啦！"）
我的晨礼服，衣领笔挺顶到下巴，

---

ᵃ 参见《圣经·传道书》第3章第1-8节："万事都有定期，天下万务都有定时：生有时，死有时；栽种有时，拔出所种的也有时；杀戮有时，医治有时；拆毁有时，建造有时；……"
ᵇ "循日劳作"：原文为古希腊赫西额德著作的标题Works and Days。这是一部著于8世纪的描绘乡下生活的长篇诗作，标题曾被译作工作与时日、劳作与时日、田功农时、农作与时日等。这里根据行文所需而译。

The Love Song of J. Alfred Prufrock

领带奢而不华,简朴的夹子衬托着它——
(她们会说:"哦他那胳臂腿多么细呀!")
45 我敢不敢
把宇宙搅乱?
一分钟内有足够时间a
一次次决定一次次修订一分钟内又推翻。

是我早已熟悉那一切,熟悉那一切:
50 熟悉那些夜晚、早晨、下午,
我已用咖啡勺把一生量出;
熟悉在消亡式降弱中消亡的语声窃窃b
淹没它的音乐来自远处的房间。
　　而我该怎样妄断?

55 我也早已熟悉那些眼神,熟悉那一切——
那眼神把你用公式般套话钉起,
当我被穿在别针上,套上公式,
当我被钉在墙上扭动不迭,
我又该怎样开始

---

a 典出莎士比亚喜剧《第十二夜》:开篇独白有"Even in a minute"感叹一切在爱情面前瞬间失却价值。
b "消亡式降弱":出典同上;开篇"That strain again! It had a dying fall(又是那个调子!有一种消亡的降弱)"之句。艾略特在《一位女士的画像》中也用到此典。

J. 阿尔弗雷德·普鲁弗洛克的情歌

60 吐掉我一日日一种种所有的残蒂？ ᵃ
  我又该怎样妄断？

我也早已熟悉那些手臂，熟悉那一切——
那些手臂带着手镯、白皙而赤裸
（但灯光之下，淡黄绒毛满胳膊！）
65 可是衣裙上的香气
让我说话这样走题？
那些手臂横陈桌面，或裹着披肩。
  我倒是该不该妄断？
  我又该怎样开始？

\* \* \* \*

70 要不要说，我曾在黄昏穿过窄窄的街巷
看到孤独男人的烟斗中升起的烟缕
他们单穿衬衫，从窗口向外探着身体？……

我真该是一双粗糙的爪子
匆匆爬过那寂静的海底。

\* \* \*

---

ᵃ 原文"butt-ends"有双关含义。有关这一行，请参见诗人《序言》诗中"The burnt-out ends of smoky days（烟雾之日的余烬）"。

88

The Love Song of J. Alfred Prufrock

75　而这下午，这夜晚，睡得这么安详！
　　修长的手指将它抚平，
　　它睡了……它累了……或许只是装病，
　　平躺在地板上，偎在你我身旁。
　　我该不该，吃罢茶水糕点和冰点，
80　有勇气把这一刻推到危机的顶点？
　　可尽管我哭泣斋戒，哭泣祈祷，ᵃ
　　尽管看到我（略秃）的头用盘子托着来到，ᵇ
　　我却不是先知——也没有大事可报；ᶜ
　　我看到我那辉煌一刻忽闪得不妙，
85　看到那永恒的侍者捧着我的外套，窃窃发笑，ᵈ
　　一句话，我就是害怕。


　　可那值不值啊，说到底，
　　就算用了杯盏，吃了橘酱，喝了茶，
　　周围瓷器环绕，还有谈论你我的闲话，
90　那值不值啊，就算
　　微笑着将事情一口咬出个决断，

---

ᵃ 见《圣经·撒母耳记下》第 12 节："而且他们悲哀哭号，禁食到晚上……"
ᵇ 《圣经·马可福音》第 6 章第 17-29 节和《马太福音》14:3-11 中讲到希律将施洗者约翰砍下来的头作为奖赏送给舞者。
ᶜ 《圣经·阿摩司书》第 7 章第 14 节中阿摩司说"我本不是先知，也不是先知的门徒。我只是一个牧人，也替人看护桑树"。
ᵈ 死神有时被称作"永恒的侍者"。拙译艾米莉·狄金森诗《未能停步等死神》对此意象有生动的描述。

把宇宙揉成了一个圆球ᵃ

把球滚向那令人窘迫的问题,

去说:"我是拉撒路,来自冥间,ᵇ

95 活过来对你表白,把一切告诉你"——

假如人家,塞个枕头在头边

  说:"我压根就不是那个用意;

  不是那回事,压根不是。"


可那值不值啊,说到底,

100 那值不值啊,就算共享过

一次次日落,一个个庭院,一条条洒水街道,

一本本小说,一只只茶杯,一条条长裙拖地——

所有这些,还有更多努力?——

我的意思根本无法说清楚!

105 但就像神灯把神经的图案投影在银幕;ᶜ

可那值不值啊,

假如人家,塞个枕头或甩掉个肩披,

然后转身面向窗口,说:

  "压根不是那回事,

110  我压根就不是那个用意。"

---

ᵃ 见本书中拙译安德鲁·马维尔诗《致他的忸怩女友》句"且把全身活力全部甜蜜/揉作一个圆球不分我你"。

ᵇ 拉撒路:耶稣把他从墓中招回人间,见《圣经·约翰福音》第 11 章第 1-44 节。

ᶜ 神灯:可以把图像放大投影到银幕上。

## The Love Song of J. Alfred Prufrock

　　　　＊　＊　＊　＊

不！我不是哈姆雷特王子，命里就不会是；ᵃ
我就是侍臣一个，我只是可以
为巡行撑个场面，弄点热闹滑稽，
给王子出个点子；确定是顺手工具，
115　恭敬而谦卑，有用很感恩，
精明而审慎，仔细且周到；
满口高谈阔论，却略显得呆钝；ᵇ
有时候，还真近乎荒唐可笑——
有时候，还真像个大傻冒。ᶜ

120　我老啦……我老啦……
穿裤子该折起裤脚啦。ᵈ

我要不要留个后分头？吃个桃子我敢不敢？ᵉ ᶠ
我要身着白色法兰绒裤，漫步在海滩。

---

ᵃ 原文"nor meant to be"，典出哈姆雷特名句"To be or not to be"，一语双关：既不该是王子，也不该"活着"。参见诗中"来自冥间"和"溺水死掉"之句。
ᵇ "高谈阔论"原文"high sentence"出自乔叟《坎特伯雷故事集》。
ᶜ 莎士比亚多部剧中有称作"the Fool"的人物，如悲剧《李尔王》中国王的忠实奴仆兼谏言人。
ᵈ 中年危机使得主人公考虑要穿时髦服装，留前卫发式。
ᵉ 前卫得有些招眼的发式。
ᶠ 很多英文作品中用到的意象"桃子"（peach）有多重含义，既指美妙事物、美人儿，在俚语中也暗指女性阴部。

J. 阿尔弗雷德·普鲁弗洛克的情歌

我听到那美人鱼在歌唱，两两相欢。a

125 我觉得她们不会对我歌唱。b

我见她们驾着海浪奔向大洋
梳理着飘向背后的浪的白发
当风把海水吹出白发和黑发。

我们徘徊着在海洋的各个房间
130 房间被海女装了红色棕色海草
直到被人声唤醒，我们溺水死掉。

(译自 T.S.艾略特 *Prufrock and Other Observations*
London: The Egoist, 1917)

---

a 参阅约翰·邓恩《歌》中 "Teach me to hear mermaids singing（教我去听美人鱼歌唱）"。
b 热拉尔·德·内瓦尔（Gérard de Nerval, 1808-55）有诗句"J'ai rêvé dans la grotte où nage la sirène（我梦见在洞中，塞壬在那里游泳）"。像《奥德赛》中的奥德修斯一样，普鲁弗洛克也听到塞壬的歌声，然而歌却不是唱给他听的。

# The Love Song of J. Alfred Prufrock

## BY T. S. ELIOT

*S'io credesse che mia risposta fosse*
*A persona che mai tornasse al mondo,*
*Questa fiamma staria senza piu scosse.*
*Ma percioche giammai di questo fondo*
*Non torno vivo alcun, s'i'odo il vero,*
*Senza tema d'infamia ti rispondo.*

    Let us go then, you and I,
When the evening is spread out against the sky
Like a patient etherized upon a table;
Let us go, through certain half-deserted streets,
5    The muttering retreats
Of restless nights in one-night cheap hotels
And sawdust restaurants with oyster-shells:
Streets that follow like a tedious argument
Of insidious intent
10   To lead you to an overwhelming question…
Oh, do not ask, "What is it?"
Let us go and make our visit.

In the room the women come and go
Talking of Michelangelo.

15 The yellow fog that rubs its back upon the window-panes,
The yellow smoke that rubs its muzzle on the window-panes,
Licked its tongue into the corners of the evening,
Lingered upon the pools that stand in drains,
Let fall upon its back the soot that falls from chimneys,
20 Slipped by the terrace, made a sudden leap,
And seeing that it was a soft October night,
Curled once about the house, and fell asleep.

And indeed there will be time
For the yellow smoke that slides along the street,
25 Rubbing its back upon the window-panes;
There will be time, there will be time
To prepare a face to meet the faces that you meet;
There will be time to murder and create,
And time for all the works and days of hands
30 That lift and drop a question on your plate;
Time for you and time for me,
And time yet for a hundred indecisions,
And for a hundred visions and revisions,
Before the taking of a toast and tea.

35 In the room the women come and go
Talking of Michelangelo.

*The Love Song of J. Alfred Prufrock*

And indeed there will be time
To wonder, "Do I dare?" and, "Do I dare?"
Time to turn back and descend the stair,
40   With a bald spot in the middle of my hair —
(They will say: "How his hair is growing thin!")
My morning coat, my collar mounting firmly to the chin,
My necktie rich and modest, but asserted by a simple pin —
(They will say: "But how his arms and legs are thin!")
45   Do I dare
Disturb the universe?
In a minute there is time
For decisions and revisions which a minute will reverse.

For I have known them all already, known them all:
50   Have known the evenings, mornings, afternoons,
I have measured out my life with coffee spoons;
I know the voices dying with a dying fall
Beneath the music from a farther room.
     So how should I presume?

55   And I have known the eyes already, known them all—
The eyes that fix you in a formulated phrase,
And when I am formulated, sprawling on a pin,
When I am pinned and wriggling on the wall,
Then how should I begin
60   To spit out all the butt-ends of my days and ways?
     And how should I presume?

J. 阿尔弗雷德·普鲁弗洛克的情歌

And I have known the arms already, known them all—
Arms that are braceleted and white and bare
(But in the lamplight, downed with light brown hair!)
65   Is it perfume from a dress
That makes me so digress?
Arms that lie along a table, or wrap about a shawl.
    And should I then presume?
    And how should I begin?

        \*   \*   \*   \*

70   Shall I say, I have gone at dusk through narrow streets
And watched the smoke that rises from the pipes
Of lonely men in shirt-sleeves, leaning out of windows?...

I should have been a pair of ragged claws
Scuttling across the floors of silent seas.

        \*   \*   \*   \*

75   And the afternoon, the evening, sleeps so peacefully!
Smoothed by long fingers,
Asleep ... tired ... or it malingers,
Stretched on the floor, here beside you and me.
Should I, after tea and cakes and ices,
80   Have the strength to force the moment to its crisis?
But though I have wept and fasted, wept and prayed,

Though I have seen my head (grown slightly bald) brought in
   upon a platter,
I am no prophet — and here's no great matter;
I have seen the moment of my greatness flicker,
85 And I have seen the eternal Footman hold my coat, and snicker,
And in short, I was afraid.

And would it have been worth it, after all,
After the cups, the marmalade, the tea,
Among the porcelain, among some talk of you and me,
90 Would it have been worth while,
To have bitten off the matter with a smile,
To have squeezed the universe into a ball
To roll it towards some overwhelming question,
To say: "I am Lazarus, come from the dead,
95 Come back to tell you all, I shall tell you all"—
If one, settling a pillow by her head
    Should say: "That is not what I meant at all;
    That is not it, at all."

And would it have been worth it, after all,
100 Would it have been worth while,
After the sunsets and the dooryards and the sprinkled streets,
After the novels, after the teacups, after the skirts that trail along
   the floor—
And this, and so much more?—
It is impossible to say just what I mean!
105 But as if a magic lantern threw the nerves in patterns on a screen:

J. 阿尔弗雷德·普鲁弗洛克的情歌

Would it have been worth while
If one, settling a pillow or throwing off a shawl,
And turning toward the window, should say:
  "That is not it at all,
110  That is not what I meant, at all."

    \*   \*   \*   \*

No! I am not Prince Hamlet, nor was meant to be;
Am an attendant lord, one that will do
To swell a progress, start a scene or two,
Advise the prince; no doubt, an easy tool,
115 Deferential, glad to be of use,
Politic, cautious, and meticulous;
Full of high sentence, but a bit obtuse;
At times, indeed, almost ridiculous—
Almost, at times, the Fool.

120 I grow old … I grow old …
I shall wear the bottoms of my trousers rolled.

Shall I part my hair behind? Do I dare to eat a peach?
I shall wear white flannel trousers, and walk upon the beach.
I have heard the mermaids singing, each to each.

125 I do not think that they will sing to me.

I have seen them riding seaward on the waves

*The Love Song of J. Alfred Prufrock*

Combing the white hair of the waves blown back
When the wind blows the water white and black.

We have lingered in the chambers of the sea
130   By sea-girls wreathed with seaweed red and brown
Till human voices wake us, and we drown.

# 《情歌》好唱口难开

这首《情歌》，不仅让其主人公 J.阿尔弗雷德•普鲁弗洛克踌躇再三，难以启口，而且对所有译者也都是很有挑战的一次翻唱。艾略特的这首成名之作同样已经有了很多前人的中文译本。这些译本虽各有千秋，但对很多语言点的理解有欠准确，在这一点上却颇多雷同；对诗歌韵律的认识和再现虽然有些试探，但也都很嫌不足。有关翻译诗歌尤其是艾略特现代诗的总体考量，即内容和形式两个方面，本书《前言》中已有陈述，这里仅就这首诗中的具体要点和翻译过程中的探索和思考讨论如下。

第 1 行："那咱就去吧"：原文"Let us go then"为什么大家一定要译作"**让我们去吧**"？你跟你的同学约着去下馆子，或者跟你的诗友相约去听歌剧，会说"让我们去……吧"么？"洋化"么？需要么？何况，"让我们去吧"这样的中文祈使句，可以理解为对"我们"之中的人发出号召的口号式文体，但更多地还可以理解为征求或乞求"我们"之外另一方的同意，而这首诗的原文中明显不存在这两种情景。诗中的"你"是主人公自我矛盾的另一面，他只是在自己说服自己，既无需请示第三方，也不必激情号召，故无用乎"让"。

4 行到 8 行：语法上，中间三行为插入成分。

《情歌》好唱口难开

9行:"聒噪":原文"argument"一词在这里指的是单方面不厌其烦的喋喋不休,因为"那些街巷一条接一条"地令人厌烦。原文为"streets that follow"而不是"streets that go paralel",而不是双方的辩论和争吵。

15行:"那黄雾的背磨蹭着玻璃窗,/那黄烟的吻磨蹭着玻璃窗":移植诗人双行末尾重复的结构。

19行:"任烟囱里落下的煤烟落在背上":英文句内重复的修辞手法译文仍加采用,虽然在中文诗歌中一般要避免。另一个例子是27行的"去备好一张脸去见你见的那些脸"。

48行:"一次次决定一次次修订一分钟内又推翻":原文"decisions and revisions which a minute will reverse"中名词的数不可不关注。我们阅读英文等外文时,对动词的时态和名词的数所表达的分量常常欠缺感受,或者无意间忽略不计,或者干脆就是浑然不觉。这种语感上的弱点很多重量级的译本也未能幸免。

52行:"在消亡式降弱中消亡的语声窃窃":原文为"voices dying with a dying fall":典出莎士比亚喜剧《第十二夜》开篇陷入相思的奥西诺公爵的"That strain again! It had a dying fall(又是那个曲调!有一股消亡的降弱)"之句。OED释义dying fall为"a fading, anticlimactic, or downbeat conclusion of something",即渐弱的、骤降的、或消沉的尾声。莎剧中dying fall同时呼应前一行中希望让爱情过饱撑死之"so die"。艾略特引用时巧妙地移植了莎翁的重叠加双关的双重修辞手段，令翻译颇费周章，既不想损失词义，又难以顺畅地再现原著的精妙——对不住了。

54 行："How should I presume"：这个 presume 很难处理：应兼有"非分设想，肆意妄想，放肆，妄作主张，贸然行事"这动脑和动手两个方面，或作"我该如何自处"。定于"妄断"，贸行妄断。

56 行：公式化断语，定式化词句，公式套话。

73 行：责备自己没出息，就该是个类似螃蟹的甲壳纲动物。

87 行："可那值不值啊，说到底"（原文 after all）："回头一想，毕竟"；是个转折关系，联系到文中的虚拟语气（就算我做了这些——其实没做——那也不一定值得呀）和普氏的反复性格，初作此译。后来主要是为了照顾韵脚，返回到"说到底"。

86-110 行：虚拟语气，定要注意。他在假设，就算有了行动，做了努力，是否值得，其实根本没有行动。译文设法把这一点表现出来。

120-124 行："我老啦……我老啦……/穿裤子该翻起裤脚啦"以及下面三行，合辙押韵，如此容易，如此顺溜，何乐而不为？

从音韵的角度看，这首诗比《荒原》有所不同：如果说后者由于写作时间在后，因而更趋向现代，所以格式也更为放得开，有更多的自由体段落，则前者受韵律诗歌影响更大，更倾向于遵守某种韵律；如果说后者是总体不讲韵律，只在特定的段落讲求韵律，则前者就是总体有韵律，尤其是在用韵方面。可以看出诗人对传统

《情歌》好唱口难开

韵律运用熟练,并善于突破韵律,灵活多变。如起始第一段,除了两行散落无韵以外,其他所有都是双行押韵:

> Let us go then, you and *I*,
> When the evening is spread out against the *sky*
> Like a patient etherized upon a table;
> Let us go, through certain half-deserted *streets*,
> The muttering re*treats*
> Of restless nights in one-night cheap *hotels*
> And sawdust restaurants with oyster-*shells*:
> Streets that follow like a tedious argu*ment*
> Of insidious in*tent*
> To lead you to an overwhelming question …
> Oh, do not ask, "What *is it?*"
> Let us go and make our *visit*.

译文照猫画虎:

> 那咱就去吧,你和我,
> 夜幕已经在天空展扩
> 像个病人麻醉在手术台;
> 咱去吧,穿过些半遭遗弃的街巷,
> 那嘈杂的可退歇的地方
> 尽是勉强熬一宿的廉价客栈
> 和到处蚝壳、满地锯末的餐馆:
> 那些街巷一条接一条
> 像居心叵测冗长乏味的呱噪
> 直把你引向一个令人窘迫的问题……

J.阿尔弗雷德·普鲁弗洛克的情歌

哦,别问"是啥呀?"
咱去探访一下吧。

也有各种四行诗的韵式,如 ABBA、ABAB、ABCB、连续若干行押同一韵,等各种排列。例如:

For I have known them all already, known them all:
Have known the evenings, mornings, afternoons,
I have measured out my life with coffee spoons;
I know the voices dying with a dying fall
Beneath the music from a farther room.
　　So how should I presume?

是我早已熟悉那一切,熟悉那一切:
熟悉那些夜晚、早晨、下午,
我已用咖啡勺把一生量出;
熟悉在消亡式降弱中消亡的语声窃窃
淹没它的音乐来自远处的房间。
　　而我该怎样妄断?

这是一个在用韵方面很典型的段落,韵式为 ABBA CC,标准的四行诗(quatrain)加一个对句(couplet)的韵式。如果进一步考察就会发现,很多段落看似松散随意,但是每一行都在韵中,很像某种诗歌格式或其变格。只在某些段落才有一两行不押韵,自由松散一下。严格地说,有些标准韵法是含有无韵行的。按照这样的标准,查整首《情歌》,几乎没有不在韵法的段落。本文对音韵的探讨，未拟深究，只在说明原文的音韵是非常齐整的，因而在译文中也应当得到相应的、等值的表达。

一首诗所用的韵律（或无韵律），无论是诗人自觉或不自觉的创作，也无论其与文字内容相关的紧密程度如何，都是诗人诗情的一种表达，都是他的诗作不可分割、不可忽略的成分，所以也都是一种内容，在翻译中都应该至少在一定程度上认作是"信"的范畴。在这个意义上，诗歌翻译的"信、达、雅"三个方面都不能脱离韵律形式而取得圆满。

# 附 录

## 当可爱的女人失足犯傻[a]

[英]奥利弗·哥尔德史密斯

当可爱的女人失足犯傻,
发现男人负心已来不及,
安抚她的忧伤有何魔法?
洗去她的眼泪有何妙计?

唯此招术能够掩盖过错,
将她的羞辱在人前藏起,
能让她那情人悔恨思过,
并绞痛他肝肠,那便是——死。

---

[a] 注:哥尔德斯密斯(Goldsmith)《威克菲尔德的牧师》中第二十四章,奥莉维亚回到自己被诱奸之地时所唱的歌。

 附录

# When Lovely Woman Stoops to Folly

## by Oliver Goldsmith

When lovely woman stoops to folly,
And finds too late that men betray,
What charm can soothe her melancholy?
What art can wash her tears away?

The only art her guilt to cover,
To hide her shame from ev'ry eye,
To give repentance to her lover,
And wring his bosom is—to die.

## 致他的忸怩女友

[英]安德鲁·马维尔

咱若天地够宽,时间够多,
小姐,这忸怩就不算罪过。
咱俩就能坐下左思右顾,
到哪整天浪漫去轧马路。
您就置身印度恒河岸边,
把那红色宝石悠然寻捡:
我在亨伯河口望潮埋怨。
灭世洪水来前爱你十年,
你自回绝此情,随你乐意,
直到犹太信徒改宗皈依。
我的痴钝爱情延延增长,
比那悠悠帝国更慢更广;
花一百年赞美你那眼睛,
凝视你的额头目不转睛;
花两百年倾慕每只酥胸,
献给玉体他处三万秋冬;
至少一世欣赏每段妙身,
最后一世打开你那芳心。
小姐,你真当得如此崇拜,
我也绝然不会降格献爱。

## 附录

可是在我背后我总听见
时间战车插翅逼近眼前；
况且在咱前方远处横卧
无穷无尽是那永恒沙漠。
你将美貌不再容颜尽丧；
石穴之中我歌不再回响；
彼时各色蛆虫将会试新
你那长久保全处子之身，
你的雅誉清名化作土屑，
我的全身情欲灰飞烟灭；
墓穴这般去处隐秘美妙，
可是我想没人在那拥抱。

因而，如今趁着青春秀色
晨露一般把你肌肤润泽，
趁着春心激情随时发动，
直如烈火涌出每个毛孔，
咱就及时行乐莫负光阴，
即刻欢爱像那怀春猛禽，
宁愿一口吞食二人时光，
不让时光咀嚼衰成枯秧。
且把全身活力全部甜蜜
揉作一个圆球不分我你，
扯着咱的欢乐猛烈奋争，
冲破生命途中铁门层层：
如此，虽然无计喝停太阳，
咱却能让太阳奔跑发光。

 附录

# To His Coy Mistress

## by Andrew Marvell

Had we but world enough, and time,
This coyness, lady, were no crime.
We would sit down, and think which way
To walk, and pass our long love's day.
Thou by the Indian Ganges' side
Shouldst rubies find; I by the tide
Of Humber would complain. I would
Love you ten years before the Flood,
And you should, if you please, refuse
Till the conversion of the Jews.
My vegetable love should grow
Vaster than empires and more slow;
An hundred years should go to praise
Thine eyes, and on thy forehead gaze;
Two hundred to adore each breast,
But thirty thousand to the rest;
An age at least to every part,
And the last age should show your heart.
For, lady, you deserve this state,
Nor would I love at lower rate.
  But at my back I always hear
Time's wingèd chariot hurrying near;

 附录

And yonder all before us lie
Deserts of vast eternity.
Thy beauty shall no more be found;
Nor, in thy marble vault, shall sound
My echoing song; then worms shall try
That long-preserved virginity,
And your quaint honour turn to dust,
And into ashes all my lust;
The grave's a fine and private place,
But none, I think, do there embrace.
   Now therefore, while the youthful hue
Sits on thy skin like morning dew,
And while thy willing soul transpires
At every pore with instant fires,
Now let us sport us while we may,
And now, like amorous birds of prey,
Rather at once our time devour
Than languish in his slow-chapped power.
Let us roll all our strength and all
Our sweetness up into one ball,
And tear our pleasures with rough strife
Through the iron gates of life:
Thus, though we cannot make our sun
Stand still, yet we will make him run.

# 译后记

我又一次站在窗前,四月了,还真有一丝春天的气息从刚刚能开到伸出一只手的窗口飘进来。天目西街稀疏的车流今日完全消失了,浦西进入全面封控。我在酒店集中隔离已近两周,顺便利用这段时间雕凿《荒原》译本;两次预定航班,两次被取消;不知何时才能回到家乡,熬过二次隔离,见到年迈的双亲。郁闷间,步古人词原韵,作《长相思·归》一阕聊表此情:

空一程,地一程,身向爷娘榻畔行,危楼暗影灯。
坐三更,卧三更,绿马河狻拼不成,倚窗寻启明。

这个四月,真是最严酷、最残忍的月份啊。联想到艾略特《荒原》所描述的颓废世界,再看如今的现实:环境毁坏,灾害频仍,瘟疫肆虐,战端重启,物欲横流,精神颓败。各种冲突愈演愈烈,被宣称终结的历史终究没有终结。文化事业自然也遭到羁绊。虽然我对于诗人的宗教情怀未必全然认同,然而其诗作在发表整一百年之后的今天,读来仍能感受其振聋发聩的警世之功效,也不枉我重温大作一回了。

全诗翻译自从完稿,过了一遍又一遍,不断探究,不断修改,一词之译,往往旬月踟蹰,字斟句酌,易稿不计其数;且从《前言》到《译后记》,可以看出,一

## 译后记

年半的时间内,也修改了一遭又一遭,时时增删,断断续续。直到今天,始告一段落。

译稿完成之后,又辗转读到恩师巫宁坤的一些文字。以前也曾听老师提到过,他那因急于归国而未完成的博士论文,研究的是艾略特,当时也没有在意;及至今天,才重新发现他的论文竟是《托·史·艾略特的文艺批评传统》,私下觉得若能得来一读,该有多好;加之我所读到的两大《荒原》译本,竟都分别出自他的师姐和挚友:我曾有幸聆听其课的赵萝蕤先生是巫宁坤老师口中"德高望重"的"大姐","一代才女",翻译家查良铮(诗人穆旦)是九叶诗派成员之一,他们都是数十年的患难之交。这也算是一点缘分。

2022 年 4 月,上海
2023 年 10 月补记,蒙特利尔

www.ingramcontent.com/pod-product-compliance
Lightning Source LLC
Chambersburg PA
CBHW031123080526
44587CB00011B/1084